Agile Business Architecture for Digital Transformation

Architectural Leadership for Competitive Business Value

Dr Mehmet Yildiz

Distinguished Enterprise Architect

First Edition, December 2019
Copyright © Dr Mehmet Yildiz
Publisher: S.T.E.P.S. Publishing Australia
P.O Box 2097, Roxburgh Park, Victoria, 3064 Australia
info@stepsconsulting.com.au
Edited by Mark Longfield

Disclaimer

Table of Contents

Contents

Chapter 1: Introduction

Purpose of this book

We are in a frenetic and a convoluted digital age. Every organisation strives to transform its business to stay competitive in this exponentially growing digital world. Digital transformation became pervasive and ubiquitous in all business ventures. This new norm of constant transformation requires architecting our business and underlying technology stacks rapidly. Establishing agile business architecture frameworks are fundamental requirements to achieve successful digital transformation outcomes.

In this book, I attempt to share my knowledge and experience using a rigorous yet agile architectural method. My aim is to add accelerated value to the broader business architecture and digital transformation communities by focusing on the practical aspect with minimal emphasis on the theoretical aspect.

The content in this book is based on my architectural thought leadership experience gained in multiple large business and enterprise architecture initiatives, focusing on business capabilities, digital transformation initiatives, and enterprise modernisation engagements, reflecting hard lessons learned in these applied settings.

In this book I attempt to redefine the role of business architects as primary leaders for digital transformation programs. The content reflects my experience and observations from the field. As a caveat, this book is not based on theories in the traditional business architecture textbooks which may conflict with my experience. My beta readers found this as a unique guide reflecting reality from the field. Hope it adds new insights for your role in the business digital transformation initiatives.

Audience

The primary audience for this book is business architects focusing on digital transformation initiatives in an accelerated way. I provided an overview of the method and framework which I developed based on my demonstrated experience in the field.

The content provided in this book can also be useful for Digital Transformation Leaders, Technical Entrepreneurs, Enterprise Architects, Technology Architects, Transformation Specialists, Program Managers, Transformation Executives including CTO-Chief Technology Officer, CDO - Chief Digital Officer, CIO -Chief Information Officer, Head of Enterprise Technologies - who engaged in and are responsible for substantial enterprise modernisation and digital transformation programs, and even Chief Marketing and Sales Officers who market and sell these initiatives in a service model.

As an educative resource, this book can also be useful for students studying in disciplines related to digital technologies, especially in MBA (Master of Business Administration), and Master of Technology programs. The book is written in a simple language address a wide variety of audience.

My Business Architecture Journey

I worked for over fifty large corporate and government organisations in the last thirty-five years. Many large companies that I work for are substantially challenged with rapid change business models, emerging technology, and increasing demands of consumers in this digital era. Every organisation that I worked for are affected by these changes. As an immediate reaction, these organisations initiated some type of modernisation and digital transformation programs at a program or the enterprise level.

These modernising and transforming organisations need new business architectural approaches to address their growing issues, imminent risks, organisational constraints, and a myriad of dependencies. The old approaches do not work for transforming organisations.

The initial modernisation and partial transformation initiatives help, to some extent, however, the focus needs to be on the new projects and initiatives to adapt and respond to the growing demands. We need integral, innovative, accelerated, and modern approaches for the emerging business requirements, growing business workloads, underlying technology, process, and tools.

Digital transformation initiatives can span across multiple business dimensions and many technology domains in large organisations. These dimensions and domains are tightly interrelated; hence, a minor change in one dimension or domain can reflect in many others. Dealing with these interrelated technology domains and moving across different business dimensions require careful considerations and substantial restructuring of myriad components.

In this book, my goal is to explain these challenges in a straightforward format methodically and in a pragmatic way providing insights based on a practical architectural approach so that my readers can deal with them effectively and in an informed way. Some of the detailed points may sound trivial or boring from a high-level business architecture perspective. However, each point I raised and explained in detail can have critical implications and make a significant impact on the success or failure of the digital transformation programs especially for responding the growing business demands and technological changes.

I want to start with a top-down business focussed approach by introducing the digital transformation method and move into the fundamentals of business architecture. In each chapter, we incrementally delve into the key framework components. Now let me introduce the method I developed and used for multiple successful digital transformation initiatives over the last decade.

The Digital Transformation Method (DTM)

The digital transformation method (DTM) that I developed covers a dozen of distinct steps to architect digital transformation initiatives. I provide you with an overview of these steps so that you can apply them to create and strengthen your business architecture frameworks aiming to support your digital transformation initiatives.

Step1: Establish Fundamentals

The first chapter covers the fundamentals. I briefly introduce the DTM starting with the essential points to help you. As the fundamentals are critical for successful architectural outcomes, the DTM starts with establishing these basic constructs using a structured and agile business architecture framework. We delve into details of these basic constructs in a distinct chapter.

Step 2: Simplify Complexity

The second step in DTM is to find innovative and accelerated ways to simplify the inherent business complexity and complicated technology landscape. Applying a modular, agile, and pragmatic business architecture framework can help you simplify this massive complexity. We have a distinct chapter to deal with this complexity using practical and proven techniques.

Step 3: Reduce Cost

The complexity of digital transformation programs poses substantial cost cases. We need to consider these detrimental cost situations at the architectural level drilling down to the design and specification levels. An effective business architecture framework, to start with, can help reduce the digital transformation cost cases from multiple angles as discussed in a specific chapter. Our business architecture can substantially contribute to reducing these substantial cost cases by taking several innovative approaches and architectural measures.

Step 4: Innovate and Invent

Digital transformation programs require an innovative and inventive mindset for business architects. We need to be creative and find new ways of doing things. Our business architecture framework plays a significant role hence must be innovative and inventive for the success of these digital initiatives.

Step 5: Collaborate Smartly

Innovation and invention happen by creating and implementing smart collaboration strategy across the digital transformation initiatives. As business architects, we need to grow a collaborative culture bringing our supporters to a single mission and joint goals. This collaborative effort can tremendously affect the success of our digital endeavours and can increase the quality of our business architecture.

Step 6: Accelerate Delivery

The next important success factor for digital transformation initiatives is maintaining a speedy delivery. To this end, we can apply agile methods and accelerated delivery mechanisms for enabling required speed. This agile approach can provide us to progress iteratively and experiment rapidly.

Step 7: Leverage Emerging Technology and Powerful Tools

Even though our focus is on the business side of the architecture, we also need to leverage emerging technology and powerful tools to succeed in our digital transformation goals. Business Architecture frameworks must factor in empowering technology and tools for the success of digital transformation programs.

Steps 8: Gain Insights from Data

The DTM focuses on business data as an empowering factor for the success of digital transformation initiatives. We need to find innovative ways to construct, reconstruct, and modernise our business data to gain insights and generate lucrative business value.

Step 8: Leverage Mobility

The next step for DTM is business and technology mobility. Our business architecture must consider the business and technology mobility requirements of the digital transformation programs. I explain the importance of mobility and how to use it effectively for architectural building blocks underlying successful digital transformation initiatives.

Step 9: Consider Smart Object

Many business organisations generate massive data coming from embedded smart objects in various devices, assets, applications, and tools of the organisation. DTM proposes the use of massive data streamed from the IoT (Internet of Things) as the major approach for generating insightful business value.

Step 10: Create High-Performance Teams

Digital transformation initiatives require high performing teams covering breadth and depth in processes, technology, and tools. Our business architecture must focus on stakeholders. Key business and technical stakeholders, especially productive team members, play important roles to achieve our transformation goals. We will delve into improving collaboration for successful business architecture supporting our digital transformation programs.

Step 11: Reuse and Repeat

Like any architectural framework, business architecture frameworks must also focus on reuse and repeatable outputs. Reusability and repeatability save us time, money, and help improve the quality of our outcomes.

These twelve steps of the DTM are involved and establish critical success factors. Therefore, we cover each step in a distinct chapter with multiple sections providing an overview and delving into details for some critical points. You can read the chapters in different orders as they suit your needs however the sections in the chapters follow a logical flow. Unless you have a specific focus on a topic for any reason, it can be useful to read each chapter in a sequential way.

Chapter 2: Business Architecture Fundamentals for Digital Transformation Programs

Purpose

The first step of our digital transformation method is establishing fundamentals. In this chapter, to establish fundamentals, we have an overview of the business architectural framework and architectural thinking approach within the context of architecting the digital transformation engagements as business architects. This is not a traditional business architecture approach. My aim here is not to teach business architecture but to highlight fundamental points that really can make a difference for your success as a business architect to lead a digital transformation program. Therefore, I tailored it for this specific context.

Understanding this new business architecture framework tailored for digital transformation context and a novel architectural thinking approach can help us establish the required fundamentals to gain digital awareness, unfold the mystery behind the business digital transformation aspirations, and increase our capabilities.

This novel, structured, and methodical approach aims to establish a high-level checklist to measure our understanding of the architectural building blocks of complex transforming business environments. As you may be aware, business systems are built-in and operate with structured patterns even though sometimes they may not be easily noticeable. From another standpoint, our brains function using structures and patterns. From these two major standpoints a structured approach to business architecture is a mandatory preposition. Business architecture is all about adding structure to chaotic business and technology situations in large business organisations aiming to modernise and transform digitally.

Using an agile and innovative business architecture framework and architectural thinking principles as a checklist can help us cover essential success factors and required steps for the success of digital transformation programs. This structured, agile, and innovative thinking process can establish the fundamentals and become invaluable for our digital transformation pursuits.

Business Architecture Framework

In order to create effective business architecture for complex digital transformation programs, we must follow an established yet innovative framework. A framework is a basic structure underlying a business and technology system. Our framework can start with understanding the organisational structure of the business. This framework can include multiple considerations and business viewpoints. Business organisations are made up of stakeholders with different roles focussing on common goals.

This point takes us to the second key component in the business architecture framework: stakeholder awareness. There may be many people with varying roles and responsibilities undertaken by the business, technical, operational, and partnering stakeholders in the digital transformation programs. It is one of our critical responsibilities to analyse our business stakeholders in a careful and methodical way. As business architects, we must precisely analyse our business stakeholders and document their roles, responsibilities, concerns, expectations, requirements, and aspirations.

Business organisations can have multiple capabilities. We can categorise these capabilities broadly under services and products offered to customers for generating revenue and growing business. Related to revenue and growth, we also need to understand the incurred costs and gained profits from these business capabilities. Our understanding of business capabilities can help us establish a fundamental business architecture framework supporting the digital transformation goals. We all know that every business must generate revenue, control costs, grow strategically, and cannot survive without profit.

Apart from business capabilities, we also need to carefully consider business value streams. Business value streams can relate to both internal and external stakeholders. External stakeholders are usually the customers of the organisation. In the simplest terms, business value streams refer to the value gained from the customers based on products and services that the business organisations provide. Business value streams are also known as business value propositions. We must analyse the value streams and map them to the future state of our business architecture framework by considering our organisation's business capabilities, vision, strategy, and tactics.

This critical focus brings us to the next significant component of the business architecture framework, which we call business vision, strategy, and tactics. These three critical business terms are interrelated. Every business initiative starts with a vision which sets the future state. Understanding business vision helps us to set business strategy. Business strategy is supported by business tactics which are small steppingstones to the strategy. These relationships amongst the vision, strategy, and tactics must be crystal clear in our business architecture framework.

The next core factor in our business architecture framework is business information. Every business organisation generates and own various information types and systems at the organisational level. Business information can include facts and can be generated from data of various systems in the organisation. In many business organisations, information not only establishes the communication and operating processes but can also be critical assets making the products and services for the customers. Therefore, business information can be considered an important capability and fundamental business value proposition for our organisation.

Our business architecture framework must consider projects and initiatives of the organisation. The main goal of these projects and initiatives is to enable business products and services for our customers. It is important to note that projects and initiatives are particularly structured, and they can be seen as practical approaches for creating our business value. Projects and initiatives manifest as products and services of the organisation. To reiterate, products and services are the major business capabilities.

Other important factors that we must consider are business events and decisions created by projects and initiatives. A business project lifecycle can consist of many business and operational events and require various business decisions related to marketing, sales, financial, political, and commercial aspects. As business architects, we need to understand these important aspects.

Our business architecture framework must also factor in governance requirements including policies, rules, and regulations. These are fundamental business management factors to govern internal and external aspect of our business and financial processes. Governance relates to all aspects of a business organisation. For example, effective stakeholder management requires flexible and functional governance model.

And last but not the least, from governance and administration perspectives, our business architecture framework must consider considerable amounts of metrics and measures to complete the full picture.

To summarise and reinforce these critical points, our business architecture framework must include organisational structure, stakeholders, business capabilities, value streams, information, vision, strategy, tactics, projects, initiatives, events, decisions, products, services, policies, rules, regulations, metrics and measures.

Now that we covered the key factors for our business architecture framework at a high level, let's focus on other fundamental aspects for our architectural practice aiming to improve the quality of our business architecture outputs. By using an architectural thinking approach, we can start with the current state and set a baseline. Analysing, understanding, and documenting the current state and creating a baseline are critical tasks to set the future state of our business architecture.

Current Business State and Baseline

To begin with, analysing, understanding and accepting our current business situation are crucial points. It doesn't matter how good or bad the situation is, we need to accept the reality 'as is' at this initial stage. Our understanding of the current business state can help us establish a tangible baseline as a starting point. Understanding and documenting the current state can depict where we are now hence can help the organisation to set business vision and strategy for digital transformation initiatives.

Compiling and establishing a demonstratable baseline of the current state in sizable business organisations can be complex and difficult, in fact most of the time, can be a daunting task for the business architects. Since there are many interrelated factors, we may be disappointed by the fact that legacy processes, systems, tools, and solutions are not integrated, not documented adequately, are managed in silos, and we cannot find any single source of truth. Therefore, we may need to conduct a substantial gap analysis and take appropriate actions to address the gaps. This is where our innovative and agile approach can come to rescue.

Despite all, we must start from somewhere to identify our current business environment and collect as much information as possible, taking various measures including picking the brains of business analysts, product specialists, technical specialists, and operational support engineers. These types of people can be resourceful and helpful for us to understand the current environment and compile a reasonable baseline. Undoubtedly, this activity can be one of the most painful exercises in the transformation lifecycle hence we shouldn't be discouraged. It is a fundamental and necessary step and pays dividends in the long run.

Now, that we highlighted the importance of understanding the current business state, let's look at the big picture and touch on another important topic called 'vision' for our business architecture framework and in our digital transformation lifecycle.

The Business Vision

Architectural thinking guides us that any new business initiative starts with a vision. In other words, based on a top-down approach, architectural thinking mandates setting the vision first. Vision is being able to think about the future with creative imagination and human wisdom for an organisation to achieve the desired business goals.

Vision sets the scene and shows us where we want to be in the future. Even though everyone has a vision, a productive and strategic vision is a business leadership capability and requires a substantial amount of intelligence, knowledge, skills, and experience. Based on my assumptions, as a business architect and digital transformation leader, you may have a fascinating vision for your organisation's transformational journey. We further enrich our vision by using an innovative and agile business architecture framework.

Practising clear vision in digital transformation engagements is necessary to think strategically. Visionary and strategic thinking can improve our business and digital intelligence. Our strategic vision must be realistic, compelling, and convincing. Strategic vision must be shared with all stakeholders and their acceptance and approval must be obtained. This is one of the crucial steps that we facilitate as a business architect in a digital transformation program.

The Strategy in Business Architecture

Once we understand the compelling business vision for our organisation's digital transformation goals, it is time to explore the business strategy. We now know where our organisation is on the digital journey and where they plan to go. The destination must be marked in the business architecture framework clearly. Our organisation's digital strategy serves as a master plan reflected in our business architecture framework. This master plan can be in the form of a high-level roadmap to take the organisations digital journey to the planned destination. Unless we have a clear strategic roadmap for the digital transformation initiative we can be easily distracted or get lost in the details and the constant noise coming from various parts of the organisation.

Visionary and strategic thinking can strengthen our business architecture framework and our digital capabilities. Our organisation's digital transformation vision and strategy can pose many requirements. Let's touch on requirements management in the digital transformation lifecycle.

Requirements in Business Architecture

As business architects working in digital transformation programs, we not only deal with the business requirements but also program requirements coming from the various project, technical, and operational domains. This means that digital transformation programs can have many requirements that business architects need to lead with architectural rigour.

Digital transformation requirements can be interrelated and have multiple facets. Most of the time, these requirements can be underestimated and seen as simple activities by the individual and siloed stakeholders; however, these requirements are not easy to manage at the program level as sometimes they can be conflicting and contradicting. This is a critical point which business architects deal with and add substantial business value.

Business architects must make concerted efforts to understand the digital transformation program requirements from all angles in structured, meaningful, and innovative ways. Dealing with requirements can involve multiple processes and stakeholders. The stakeholders can be from different parts of the organisation with varying goals, roles, and responsibilities. We need to identify them, reach consensus for varying views, and find effective ways to integrate them. The processes can be convoluted, ambiguous, and fragmented.

Business initiatives, projects, users, information, data, and systems have their standard and unique requirements. For example, there are different requirements for different kinds of users. Internal and external users, technical, executive, and management users can pose different requirements. Business, systems, and organisational data also can have their unique requirements. The way to turn data to information, and information to knowledge can pose multi-dimensional requirements.

The system requirements can be categorised under technical, support, and operational requirements. Broadly speaking, in architectural terms, requirements can be classified under two main categories, namely, functional and non-functional. This simple categorisation can help us analyse requirements in a contextual manner.

The functional requirements involve what a business system offers to the consumers as functionality. For example, the business system may offer calculations, data processing, or business workflow management. Functional requirements usually relate to consumers of business solutions. They describe what consumers expect from business products and services.

Non-functional aspects of the requirements focus on quality. We abbreviate them as NFRs. The purpose of NFRs is to focus on how business solutions can accomplish business functionalities, such as their performance, availability, security, reliability, scalability, usability, configuration, scalability. These are primarily technical and operational requirements to increase the quality of business solutions. NFRs set by business stakeholders and addressed by the technical support and maintenance teams.

Requirements gathering for digital transformation programs are an end to end process. This process covers activities such as collecting, analysing, clarifying, tracking, validating, and using them. As practical guidance, we use the acronym SMART to characterise the validity and quality of requirements.

SMART stands for specific, measurable, actionable, realistic, and traceable. Careful consideration of these five attributes, as guiding principles, can help us improve the quality of requirements management.

To better understand the business requirements, especially from the users' perspective, we must analyse and understand the use cases.

Use Cases in Business Architecture

In conjunction with analysing requirements, understanding the use cases in the digital transformation programs sets the essential architectural rigour required from the business architects. Dealing with business use cases require different thinking modes, such as emphatic thinking which is looking at things from the user's perspective. Observing with empathy is a critical skill for business architects.

A use case is a specific situation depicting the use of a product or service of a business solution by the consumer. We develop use cases from the users' perspective. Therefore, we must understand the intention of consumers aiming to use a particular component or specific aspect of a solution building block.

Usually, the functional requirements can be used to formulate the business use cases. Alternatively, in some circumstances, use cases can help formulate the functional requirements. This means that the use cases and the functional requirements are interrelated. We must analyse them together; not in isolation.

A group of selected and representative users can help us understand the use cases when we interact with them in the requirements gathering phase. We can ask open-ended questions to these users and obtain their feedback on how they intend to use a specific business function.

In general, business use cases need to be defined and elaborated with the input from all stakeholders of the business solution; not just end-users. There may be different use cases for different stakeholders in the digital transformation programs.

Use cases can also be determined based on roles and personas. The term persona represents a fictitious character based on our knowledge of the user. Identifying personas and use of them in our use case development and requirements analysis can be beneficial for communicating requirements and identified use cases to various stakeholders.

While dealing with use cases, refinement of the requirements continues as a parallel activity in the subsequent phases. We must ensure to follow a pragmatic approach to the requirements handling phase. Let's be mindful that a perfectionist approach to requirements handling can consume a large amount of our limited budget, which is common and undesirable situation experienced in many failed digital transformation initiatives.

Once we handled the requirements at a reasonable amount and integrate them with identified use cases of the digital transformation initiatives, we can move into setting the current and future state as a critical architectural artefact of our organisation's digital transformation initiative.

Current and Future State

Once we understand the requirements and clarify the use cases of the digital transformation initiative, we can analyse them within the current state context. The current state architectural description can show us where we are now in this journey.

By understanding the current state, its requirements and the use cases to transform the initiative, we can set the future state and develop a roadmap to reach the target transformation goals. The future state requires a substantial amount of analysis and detailed predictions. In the future state phase, we can consult multiple subject matter experts to ensure the future state reflects the vision, mission, and architectural strategy; and ensure that our predicted future state meets identified business requirements and the use cases.

This methodical approach of understanding the current environment and setting the future state is a fundamental architectural activity which can be applied to any digital transformation initiative that we engage on as business architects. This essential approach is instrumental for the success of our digital transformation initiatives. Once we set the future state agreed and approved by the key stakeholders, our next critical step in the lifecycle is to assess the feasibility of the solution for its construct, deployment, and consumption goals.

Architectural Feasibility for Business Outcomes

An architectural method can guide us to think and determine the feasibility of our digital transformation roadmap by examining the risks, dependencies, assumptions, and the constraints on the way.

We can determine the feasibility of the roadmap using a viability assessment work-product in any architectural method. Viability assessment work-product is a template covering all aspects of our business solution particularly from its useability, consumption, and operability perspectives. We can either use a viability assessment work-product template from an established method such as TOGAF or our organisation's proprietary method.

One cautious note is that the viability assessment can be categorised under different names. To ensure, we can check which work-product is used in our proprietary method to capture risks, issues, assumptions, constraints, and dependencies.

Developing a comprehensive viability assessment can help us mitigate critical risks, resolve existing issues, validate assumptions, address challenging constraints, dependencies, and complex interdependencies. Missing this critical step in our digital business transformation lifecycle can result in dire consequences especially in the long run when the products and services are in use. Therefore, producing a well analysed, agreed, and approved viability assessment work-product is a mandatory step in the business architecture lifecycle of a digital transformation initiative.

Most of the time, assessing viability also require making a considerable number of trade-offs to reach optimal outcomes. Let's understand what an architectural trade-off is.

Architectural Trade-offs

When architecting business digital transformation initiatives, we may need to make substantial amounts of trade-offs. When making trade-offs, we must consider critical factors, such as cost, quality, functionality, usability, and several other non-functional items including capacity, scalability, performance, usability, and security.

We make trade-offs to create a balance between two required yet incompatible items. In other words, a trade-off is a compromise between two options. For example, it is possible to make a trade-off between quality and cost for particular items.

Sometimes, dealing with trade-offs can pose a dilemma. We may tear ourselves between two competing and compelling options. In these circumstances, we must revisit our priorities. Re-examining our priorities, especially set by the key stakeholders for the business objectives, can provide us useful clues and necessary guidance. In addition, we can also revisit our approved vision, mission, and architectural strategy as sometimes our memories may fail to remember exact details in the rapid-paced transforming business environments.

There may also be times that we make some of the architectural trade-offs to deal with uncertainties and ambiguities. To deal with these types of trade-offs, we can use techniques such as comparing, combining, and contrasting situations, and taking calculated risks.

It is not possible to develop a business architecture framework without taking risks in any sizeable digital transformation program. It is also possible that these risks can be turned into opportunities hence we need to mitigate them methodically and measurably. Now let's discuss the next critical point covering architectural decisions.

Architectural Decisions

Each trade-off that we make for any digital transformation construct must be supported by solid architectural decisions. These crucial architectural decisions can have substantial business implications for the success or failure of our digital transformation initiatives.

We must create architectural decisions very carefully, measurably, and agreeably. The main reason for this each architectural decision can have a severe impact and multiple implications on the business outcomes. Another reason is that changing the architectural decisions at later phases of the lifecycle can be very costly, time-consuming, and chaotic.

Some implications of architectural decisions can be cost-related, compliance constraints, while others can relate to non-functional aspects such as performance, scalability, capacity, availability, security, and usability.

In addition, our architectural decisions must be validated with subject matter experts and communicated with multiple stakeholders for their acceptance and approval to reach the optimal consensus on the validity of the decision.

The context for Business Architecture

After creating the architectural decisions, reaching consensus, and obtaining necessary approvals, the next challenging task is to provide a representative picture of the architectural framework for digital transformation initiative in a single page. This illustrated representation is usually called the system context showing the architectural framework with critical dependencies. System context is a work-product template which can be found in many established methods as a sample.

Creating a system context requires abstraction skills. This means that we need to represent a large volume of information in a small diagram by setting concise relationships amongst the system components in the architectural framework. We can apply the proverbial principle of 'a thousand words in a single picture'.

This abstract thinking skill is an example of our architectural intelligence that we can add to the digital transformation initiative process. Setting the context for the framework can help us communicate it to relevant stakeholders in a common and understandable manner. In short, the system context adds clarity to understanding the proposed architectural framework for digital transformation initiative.

Models for Business Architecture

We need to develop multiple architectural models for digital transformation initiatives. Models are essential work-products in the business architectural framework. A model is the proposed structure typically on a smaller scale than its original.

Once we draft a specific architectural framework at an abstract level and our stakeholders understand and approve it, the next important step in the architectural thinking process is to represent the details in an abstract level by describing each building block and their relationships.

Describing details in abstract representations requires a great deal of thinking and mental exercise, including dealing with multiple patterns, which can stimulate our architectural thinking abilities. Many business architects enjoy this intellectual practice admired by business stakeholders.

As business architects we need to develop multiple business-related architectural models. For example, we can follow the TOGAF method, to customise the following models for our needs: Business Context, Business Capabilities, Value Streams, Data Context, and IT context. These are essential models every business architect needs to be familiar with. I choose not to go into details of preparing these models as they are fundamental skills possessed by the business architects. For those starting the business architecture recently, reviewing the work-product templates for these models from various business architecture methods can be useful.

In addition, considering we lead the digital transformation program as business architects, we may need to create or help with the creation of some of the vital and generic architectural models which we can apply to the potential modernisation and transformation initiatives. The fundamental models that we must consider are Component Model, Operational Model, Performance Model, Security Model, Availability Model, Services Model and Cost Model. Usually, rather than developing these models, we provide input to the relevant architecture team members who may be directly responsible for authoring these model work-products.

We must ensure that these models are precisely documented, reviewed by the domain architects, and governed by the Architecture Board or a Design Authority in the organisation or digital transformation program level. You can find samples of these models in established methodologies searching the names provided in the previous paragraph.

Documentation of the architectural models can include both textual explanations and practical diagrams. For example, for a Component Model, all components and their relationships can be clearly illustrated in a diagram. The components and their functions can also be explained in detail in a document. Some architects may need to use their proprietary architectural tools or even a PowerPoint based on the document requirements of the program. I commonly use MS Visio as a tool to create my Component and Operational Models and share the output as a PDF to the relevant stakeholders.

The architectural diagrams can be useful communication tools for the selected models in the program because the governance process for handling the architecture models requires presenting them to the Architecture Board or a Design Authority.

With an effective presentation and articulated communication, obtaining technical assurance approvals can be faster and easier. Otherwise, people in these forums struggle to understand the key points and consume substantial amounts of time to approve them. Applying agile principles to the architectural review process is a critical success factor for digital transformation programs.

Approval for some of these models may also need to be obtained from the financial, commercial and other business stakeholders. For example, the Cost Model, the Services Model, and the Availability Model can have special content that may require financial or commercial approval at the program and the enterprise level.

As business architects, we not only deal with the architectural and technical aspects of the digital transformation initiatives but also the financial and commercial aspects. We also need to collaborate with multiple architects in transformation programs. These collaborating architects can create several models using the best architectural practices in the digital transformation program and we guide and support them strongly.

High-Level Designs Guided by Business Architecture Framework

Once the architectural models are developed, we need to create or help with the creation of fundamental high-level designs for the program. Digital transformation initiatives require the development of multiple work-products covering high-level designs based on the architectural context that we discussed in the previous sections.

Use of fundamental high-level designs aiming to see the big picture for each solution building block can be instrumental for the success of digital transformation initiatives. The high-level designs must be well understood, accepted, and approved by relevant stakeholders. As a word of caution, let's be mindful that at the later stages of the digital transformation lifecycle, it can be difficult and very costly to change these high-level designs since the many detailed activities of the initiatives are built on the guidance provided in these high-level designs.

To comply with this critical point, we must ensure that the high-level designs are produced using business vision, organisational strategy, initiative requirements, use cases, architectural decisions, system context, and the overall digital transformation roadmap. These high-level designs must fully be aligned for reaching the goals of the optimal digital transformation outcomes.

Detailed Designs and Specifications

I know you would ask how does detailed designs and specifications relate to business architecture. Let's remember the context of this book is about leading the architecture of digital transformation programs. Like any other enterprise IT system, the modernisation and transformation initiatives are expected to deliver all their detailed designs and specifications correctly. To this end, as business architects, applying a comprehensive configuration management practice for digital transformation constructs and components are essential architectural practice for an end to end success of the programs.

In digital transformation initiatives, specifications can be defined as the act of precisely identifying, configuring, and documenting the constructs in the transforming ecosystem. Since specifications require precision and deep practical engagement, delivering the right specification is an essential requirement for transforming applications, underlying infrastructure, and their critical business and emergency responses to the consumers.

Architectural, business, application, and system specifications must be accurate, reliable, and fast for collecting data, disseminating information, sharing data across multiple components, and making data-driven decisions for the business outcomes. Unreliable configuration and communication of the specifications caused by various silos in the organisation, wrong configurations, unreliable decisions made by those specifications, and the cumbersome layout in the user interface documentation can lead to disastrous results when attempting to detail and make the digital transformation solutions operable for consumption.

Finding inaccurate detailed designs or wrong specifications during the implementation and production support phase can be very cost-prohibitive due to massive re-work requirements. These unexpected errors shatter the whole digital transformation initiative from every angle, hence as business architects supporting digital transformation initiatives, we can be the first ones who kept responsible for the dire consequences.

In addition, rework implications for service level agreements can cause considerable amounts of financial loss to the business organisation. From my experience, rework has been identified as one of the most critical lessons learned from the failed digital transformation initiatives. Therefore, we must ensure the detailed designs and related specifications for transformation constructs are accurate and verified by relevant subject matter, portfolio, and domain experts.

As lead business architects responsible for digital transformation initiatives in our organisation, we may set and chair the design authority with input from the enterprise architects for the digital transformation programs. To run successful design authority forums, we must closely work with the solution architects, domain architects, technical specialists, and solution designers. We cannot afford any silos in high-level, detail design, and specification phases of the digital transformation lifecycle. The architectural approach must be fully integrated as an entire high functioning collaborative team under our business, technical, and architectural leadership.

Governance for Digital Transformation

Business, architectural, and technical governance are critical aspects of digital transformation initiatives. Complex digital transformation programs require particular governance model due to their demanding nature. Therefore, a dynamic and flexible governance model must be applied to digital transformation initiatives.

The traditional stringent and extreme rule-based, punitive, or oppressive governance models can be roadblocks to the progress of digital transformation initiatives. From my experience, agile principles best suit to apply dynamic governance models. We further discuss the agility point in the chapter titled "Accelerate Delivery".

Governance committees in digital transformation programs can be complicated and sophisticated at multiple levels. There are many roles and responsibilities for these governance committees. For example, business architects can lead the overall digital initiatives using an overarching business framework, transformation architects can run the architecture review boards or the design authority forums established for complex digital transformation programs. Usually enterprise architects focus on compliance across the enterprise reflected in the digital transformation program.

Domain architects, technical specialists, and many subject matter experts representing multiple domains can verify technical accuracy in their specific disciplines and expertise areas. There may also be multiple other professionals attending the governance forums for various business reasons.

For example, sponsoring executives can join these governance forums every now and then and mainly facilitate the financial and commercial aspects of the digital transformation initiatives. Program managers, most of the time, attend every governance forum for the program and they are responsible for the compliance and risk management of the particular initiatives under their leadership.

We can apply different governance frameworks based on our industry and the solution domains. For example, one of the common frameworks for technical governance in the industry is COBIT (Control Objectives for Information and related Technology). Use of frameworks like COBIT can help business organisations gain optimal value from their IT investments by maintaining a balance between gaining business value, optimising risk levels and resource use. There can be other governance model based on the industry which our business organisation belongs to and must adhere for compliance purposes.

Now is the time to conclude the overview of architectural fundamentals that we can use in our twelve-step digital transformation method. In the next chapter, we delve into the details of the next step, digital complexity, which is another important topic related to digital transformation initiatives.

Chapter 3: Business Complexity

Purpose

After the fundamentals, the second pillar in our digital transformation method (DTM) is dealing with business complexity within digital transformation context. Dealing with business complexity requires extensive architectural capability and substantial business input to digital transformation initiatives.

Considering the context of digital transformation, the purpose of this chapter is to point out the complexity as one of the most significant challenges related to the successful outcome of digital transformation initiatives. To this end, we must find innovative ways to architect simplicity in the program.

Once we understand the complexity and embrace it as a reality, the next step is to find effective ways to deal with complexity. As you may guess already, from an architectural standpoint, I'd propose a methodical, structured, integrated, and agile approach to deal with complexity. Let's deep dive to explore this critical architectural challenge!

Enterprise Business Environments

We know that business organisations can be extremely complex with challenging business requirements, voluminous of data, intricate information systems, multiple layers of underlying systems, subsystems, technology stacks, myriad of tools, a growing number of applications, and cumbersome processes coupled with numerous stakeholders with different agendas and consumers with different expectations. You got the picture!

Even though systems, applications, data, information, tools, processes, and technology stacks can be challenging, the more significant part of the iceberg, the real challenge, is dealing with people in the enterprise, especially multiple stakeholders with different roles, responsibilities, confusing and conflicting agendas.

As a result of this situation, coupling business systems and stakeholders can add extra complexity to the organisation's business landscape and environments. Therefore, as business architects, we must find effective ways to manage enterprise complexity for our digital transformation initiatives.

Managing Complexity

Fortunately, there are various approaches and techniques to manage complexity in business organisations transforming to digital vision. In this section, as a jumpstart, I provide a generic approach commonly used by business architects to deal with digital transformation complexity.

The most common technique which we can use is simplifying complexity by using a partitioning approach. This technique applies to both business systems and stakeholders. To simplify complexity, we can divide, subdivide, segregate, or apportion the systems, objects, components, or teams to smaller units.

The process of partitioning refers to making smaller parts of an astronomical object like a digitally transforming business organisation. Let's say that we are dealing with an extensive infrastructure network system in the business organisation. Dealing with such an extensive system can be daunting. In this case, we partition the overall network to smaller parts such as a wide-area network, a metropolitan network, a local-area network, or wireless network. Then we can further partition the wide-area network from tools and technology stacks perspectives such as routers, switches, bridges, hubs, and other devices. Then, dealing with the segmented system can be simpler, more efficient, and faster.

Once we partition an overarching system, then we can start simplifying it by looking at its size and quantity. An effective way of simplifying a system can be performed by reducing the size or number of repetitive constituents. Take the number of servers in the underlying infrastructure, for example. Dealing with a thousand units of servers or just ten servers can make a massive difference for complexity. Reducing numbers or sizes can be useful to simplify quantitative aspects of the systems and their components.

Another technique that we can apply could be moving an item from a large group of the clustered items, but still, keep the relationship to preserve its core identity in the cluster. We touch on the importance of simplification for digital transformation initiatives as a critical success factor in the subsequent sections of this chapter.

After partitioning and simplifying, another useful method that we can apply is iterating it. Probably, you heard a lot about this term while working with agile methods and in agile scrum teams. It is a buzzword in agile scrum teams. Iteration can be defined as progressing activities in smaller steps and chunks continuously. Iteration can be considered as one of the best-proven approaches to deal with complexity and uncertainty.

Moving with iterative steps, especially in digital transformation programs, we can achieve some small and fast results. Then, if the small result is positive, we can make quick progress and go to the next iteration. If the result is negative, we fail quickly but learn how not to do this specific action and try another iteration for success. It can be viewed as in the analogy of babies to learn walking experientially.

The positive side of this negative result is that we fail cheap, and we fail quickly. Failing cheap and quickly don't make a big negative difference from financial, commercial, or project schedule perspectives. Paradoxically, failing cheap and quick provide financial gains especially in complex digital transformation programs. We can learn quickly, deal with uncertainties efficiently, and move faster to create better results for our digital transformation goals.

Using a quick memory trick, we can remember these three basic methods with the following analogy. We have separate teams for different functions at work; this is partitioning of teams. We only belong to a single nation; this is a reductive simplification. We plan for a school or certification exam chapter by chapter; this is iteration. There are also various process and approaches that we apply for these techniques. We cover them in the subsequent sections of this chapter.

Simplicity for Digital Transformation

Simplicity is a substantial requirement to be fulfilled for digital transformation and modernisation initiatives. Provision of simplicity is also one of the critical attributes of business architects and digital transformation leaders. Professionals dealing with digital transformation initiatives must be capable of turning complexity to simplicity.

Simplicity is required and touches almost every angle of digital transformation initiative, as these initiatives can incredibly be complex. Simplicity, in sophisticated business organisations, is a paradoxical topic. Digital transformation initiatives are complex endeavours and require sophisticated intelligence, capabilities, in-depth knowledge, varied skills, and extensive experience. We must simplify the complicated processes, systems, tools and technologies using our business understanding and architectural capabilities.

Paradoxically, to create simplicity, one must deal with a lot of complexity, complications, and sophisticated matters. As lead business architects, this is where our business knowledge and architectural capabilities play an essential role in digital transformation initiatives. Obtaining the essential business knowledge, acquiring advanced methodical skills, and gaining substantial experience for the multiple business domains are not easy tasks and not indeed trivial activities. We need to deal with complexity using our business and digital intelligence to create simplicity within the digital transformation program.

From my observations, digitally intelligent business architects who deal with complexity and sophisticated matters can have extraordinary attributes to simplify situations for the stakeholders of the digital transformation programs. At the most fundamental level, we know that creating simplicity requires effective communication at all levels.

Creating and maintaining simplicity is a well sought-after characteristic for digital business services and products. Many business organisations and the modern digital world aim to offer simplified solutions to their consumers. As opposed to complexity, simplicity is naturally favourable by digital service consumers. Therefore, digital transformation leaders are expected to simplify complex situations and complicated problems, hence offer simple solutions to the consumers. Communication simplicity is one of the critical factors; hence, we touch on and emphasise it in the next section.

Communication Simplicity for Digital Transformation

As business architects focussing on digital transformation initiatives, we are expected to articulate the most complicated and complex matters in a simple format that is understandable by all stakeholders of the initiatives. This is a fundamental business, professional, architectural, and technical capability.

Creating simplicity for communication requires in-depth knowledge, flexible thinking, and demonstrated skills, and expertise in articulation. Creating and maintaining simplicity requires crystal clear communication at all levels. One way of clear communication is to customise our message to stakeholders' level in the right context. This condition requires thinking on our feet at all times.

Creating and maintaining simplicity is not only a desired attribute for dealing with business, architectural, and technical matters but also building relationships with the business stakeholders. We must communicate in simple terms with our stakeholders by refraining from convoluted sentences, technical jargons, and myriad of acronyms. Many business stakeholders dislike frequent acronym using business architects. Let's beware of this undesirable situation in our digital transformation programs when dealing with our stakeholders.

When we use an acronym, we always should provide the meaning of the acronym to maintain clarity and remove obscurity. We cannot assume that our stakeholders are capable of understanding every acronym that comes to our mind during the conversations. Some stakeholders can be intimated by the use of acronyms and can struggle to maintain conversations in the right direction hence we need to be mindful of this situation.

As business architects, we must simplify business, architectural, and technical matters when dealing with technical issues in various forums of the digital transformation programs. One way of simplifying architectural and technical matters is the use of metaphors with practical examples.

We must establish relationships with our stakeholders that depict simplicity and efficiency in the program. This simplified and effective communication approach can make us more credible and create a perception of trustworthiness hence can help us communicate our message more effectively and efficiently.

User-Centric Simplicity

Apart from stakeholder communication, creating and maintaining simplicity with the users or consumers is critical. Creating and maintaining user-centric simplicity requires to ask the question of how we can create products and services simple, intuitive, and human-centric. The consumer-oriented simplicity is a requirement for leading innovative teams in the digital transformation initiatives.

As mentioned in the previous section, as business architects and digital leaders, possessing these credentials, we need to motivate our teams to think in simple user-centric terms when conveying our messages for complicated business, architectural, and technical processes.

We must understand that the path to digital transformation begins with simplifying the business systems, tools, technology, and process components at all levels and layers. User centricity is a critical success factor in achieving this goal.

One of the effective ways to simplification in a digital transformation program for user-centricity is automating routine tasks and repetitive technology stacks mandated by our business architecture framework. Automation can help standardise and simplify convoluted and repetitive tasks and procedures prone to human errors. In the simplest terms and the most basic level, reducing human errors can increase consumer satisfaction. While delving into details in architecture and technology, we also need to focus on emerging business needs by simplifying them in consumer terms.

In general, business consumers keep complaining that architecture and technology create complexity and make it difficult to understand concepts and objects in natural human language. For example, many consumers complain about the cumbersome documentation written in a convoluted language.

I witnessed that some consumers also show their disapproval for voluminous of documents for the use of a small technology device for achieving simple business goals. They call it a waste as most of the time they ignore them. We need to be mindful of providing concise information in the right context and business use cases in our digital transformation initiatives.

Process Simplicity for Digital Transformation

Process simplicity is a crucial activity that we must deal with as business architects. We can start with the organisational, cultural, and user point of views at the program level aligned with the enterprise goals. This business, cultural, and user-oriented approach can be a good starting point to tackle our convoluted processes.

From a cultural standpoint, there appears to be a generational disconnect in dealing with processes in numerous business organisations. For example, older business users used to read manuals to solve their computer problems. In the past, software stacks used to come with large read-me files. There were hundreds of pages of process documents that they needed to go through.

However, the new generation in these business organisations appears to work with technology intuitively. These young employees hardly look at product or process manuals. If they are stuck, they would usually watch a YouTube video on how to do something or how to troubleshoot a problem. Instead of reading process documents, they prefer watching a video and resolve issues experimentally. Considering these shifts in the culture of business organisations, we need to be mindful of trends in business practices, and consumer technologies, hence simplify and modernise our processes based on evident consumer trends.

We must have a specific mission to simplify the business and technology processes and make them user-centric. This effort aims at efficiency and effectiveness of technology products and services provided by our digital transformation initiatives.

Architectural and technology simplification are other critical points that we must consider while addressing process modernisation guided by the business architecture framework. Architectural practices and technology are rapidly transforming towards service orientation. Most of the architecture and technology domains are provided based on modular services models.

Within the digital transformation context, the most common architectural shift and technology trend is the Cloud services model. In the Cloud services model, everything is provided as services. For example, cloud service models can be a business environment, underlying infrastructure, integrating platforms, data and software as services. Indeed, many other technology stacks and processes such as data analytics and business processes can be offered as simplified services. In other words, everything can be provided as a service in the Cloud service model.

The sophisticated services model in the back office of the business organisations requires substantial amounts of simplification for users to take benefits of using complicated technology offerings. We can add value to our business organisation by simplifying the processes of these services for consumers of our product and services manifested by our digital transformation programs.

We must motivate and inspire our architectural and design team members to simplify process documents by empathising with our consumers. Simplification is an innovative process that we must lead as role model business architects.

Simplicity and clarity are closely related concepts. Especially in the digital services industry, providing a transparent experience to the stakeholders and consumers are desirable attributes. Besides, making this transparent experience available to the end-user even more simplified and more explicit formats by providing clear usage patterns can add additional value to our digital service provision goals.

An effective way of simplifying our processes and providing simplicity to the consumer is to think like the consumers. We must keep focusing on the core tenets of simplifying the process of our products and services for the best possible user experience and satisfactory consumption merits.

Design Simplicity for Digital Transformation

As business architects, we can motivate and inspire our digital transformation designers to create and maintain simplicity in design activities. Design simplicity plays an essential role in the success of digital transformation initiatives. Design simplicity may have a tremendous impact on the subsequent phases of the digital transformation lifecycle, such as for service delivery and support phases. The simpler the designs are, the more effective the delivery and service support can be.

Applying design thinking practice, combined with adopting agile methods for design activities, can be effective simplification approaches in the digital transformation programs. As a business value proposition, design simplification can be seen as an enabler of accelerated digital service delivery. Design thinking practices and the agile delivery methods strive for simplifications mandating the use of iterative and experimental approaches. Progressing our digital transformation pursuits with iterations can be simpler than progressing monolithically with whole chunks.

By applying design thinking practice and agile methods to the design phase of the digital transformation initiatives, complicated business requirements and solution processes can be simplified using simple use cases based on personas, user stories, retrospectives, and user empathy maps, hence the potential design flaws can be addressed rapidly.

By using design thinking practice and an agile approach, complex systems can be deconstructed to smaller parts and dealt with the use of simpler chunks. We can simplify system relationships with iterative progress. Our simplification focus on design activities for digital transformation initiatives must be on smaller building blocks in an iterative manner.

Most of the business services nowadays are digitally offered to consumers using mobile devices such as tablets and smartphones. Therefore, our mobile design activities must focus on simplicity by removing clutter from user screens due to the natural capabilities of small screen views. These types of design constructs must focus on only fundamentally essential objects for consumer use. These design constructs and relevant constraints must be fundamental considerations for achieving our user-focused digital transformation goals.

Designing complex business systems, products, and services may also require considerable amounts of simplification activities through modular and service-oriented design mechanisms. Modularity and modular approaches for dealing with complex digital transformation initiatives are essential considerations for design simplification, business process modernisation, and digital transformation goals.

One of the approaches for the digital transformation goals in design simplification can be a domain-based walkthrough of simplifying modules of, business architecture, business applications, underlying infrastructure, middleware, security, network, and data domains.

To elaborate on design simplification in the technology domain, let's take the recent design constructs of the microservices and containers in the Cloud services model as an example. Microservices and containers can break down monolithic interdependent architecture constructs into manageable, and independent building blocks. A container in the Cloud services model, as a loosely coupled system, can be an entire runtime environment in a service bundle. It can include dependencies, binaries, libraries, and configuration files. These new techniques and approaches can help us simplify the essential design processes for digital transformation initiatives.

As business architects, we must be conscious of design simplicity for our digital transformation initiatives and work with our designers closely to create desirable business value. To achieve this business goal, we can run workshops to convey the business value message for creating intuitive user-centric designs based on well-sought-after simplicity principles. As business architects, we usually don't practice design activities hands-on, however, as architectural leaders in the digital transformation programs, we facilitate design activities demonstrating our informed and guiding leadership.

Specification Simplicity for Digital Transformation

Dealing with business and technical specifications can be seen a very low-level task for business architects however in digital transformation initiatives we must guide for creating and maintaining the simplicity of business and technical specifications. Convoluted specifications can be troublesome and may require substantial simplification process for digital transformation goals. To this end, we can engage multiple business domain specialists, subject matter experts, domain and solution architects to help us to simplify business and technical specifications in the digital transformation program.

For many years, in traditional business settings, we spent substantial time and energy on the system and user specification of products and services. As documented in the body of knowledge for business architecture, enterprise architecture, and business transformation initiatives, creating voluminous of business and technical specifications with many engineers, architects, and technical specialists incurred substantial cost an enormous amount of funds for business organisations. However, it has been documented that the investment made on these convoluted specifications yielded no gain or minimal gain.

The modern digital transformation trends, mobile user culture, and applying agile principles to specification handling made substantial changes in addressing the cumbersome specifications, especially concerning the users or consumers. According to the recent industry analyst reports, intricate and in-depth technical details for user specifications are found unnecessary. We know that the agile principles propose simplifications of cumbersome specifications delivered in user stories format.

User stories are simple templates, including the functionalities, capabilities, and specifications obtained from users' or consumers' point of views. Developing and understanding the user stories, usually consist of a single page, can be much more comfortable and more effective than developing or disseminating hundreds of pages of specifications in traditional methods.

Business and Technical Language Simplicity for Digital Transformation

As business architects, we deal with business and technical language to communicate with our stakeholders in digital transformation initiatives. Creating and maintaining simplicity for the use of business and technical language to convey architectural messages in digital transformation programs are paramount. Effective business and technical communication require substantial simplification at the architectural level. The simplification process for business and technical communication can enable to facilitate understanding of issues, risks, and dependencies for business, architectural, and technical matters effectively.

Simplified business and technical communication can be challenging due to their complex nature. However, we can apply specific rules and techniques to address these concerns. As business architects, using abstraction, conceptions, and context-specific techniques, we can translate complex issues into clear messages that can be acted on or executed with simplicity and agility in the digital transformation programs.

Refraining from convoluted business jargons and technical phrases, instead, using precise business-oriented language with explicit technical terms are essential factors for clear communication. Even though we may have an extensive business vocabulary and a broad range of technical terms, particularly in-depth knowledge of architectural and technical matters, we need to be able to use simple language to pass our message to our non-technical stakeholders and users.

We can customise our message by using common terms and references based on the target group profile. For example, while speaking to a manager, a secretary, an executive, a salesperson, and a technician, we use their vernacular. We can customise our message based on a stakeholder profile in a specific context. This means that while we can use advanced business terms to senior executives to articulate a point, we can use technical terms to talk with engineers, subject matter experts, or technical specialists. This stakeholder awareness, customisation, and flexibility in communication are critical success factors to convey our message across the digital transformation program.

We also need to be aware that the attention span for our generation is relatively low due to many digital disruptions in our lives. To this end, while conveying a critical message, we must get to the point quickly before losing the attention of our stakeholders. For example, we can use lively words to illustrate a complex architectural and technical situation rather than using abstract terms and jargons.

Moreover, simplicity in written business and technical communication is a critical success factor. Business stakeholders usually don't have much time and brainpower to understand intricate details in our documents with convoluted technical terms, jargons, and acronyms. When authoring a business architecture document for a digital transformation initiative, we must be sharp and to the point with clear statements. As a principle, short sentences are always preferable to improve readability and hold attention span for our audience.

The main benefit of simplification for oral and written business and technical communication is to pass the desired message effectively in the shortest possible time. Therefore, as a principle, it is critical to refrain from jargons, acronyms, big words, and complex sentence structures both in verbal and written communication in the digital transformation programs.

Besides, being able to articulate the business, architectural, or technical situation in the simplest possible terms can also increase the confidence of the stakeholders in the digital transformation programs. Practising and demonstrating this capability are essential success factors for our digital transformation goals.

A well balanced qualitative and quantitative context in simplifying the business, architectural, technical language is also essential. We can balance qualitative and quantitative aspects while conveying a technical message to a broader audience in the program. To achieve this goal, we must be context-aware and deliver our message in the right context for both qualitative and quantitative situations.

We need to strive to articulate the business value proposition to the business stakeholders rather than showing off our architectural and technical eminence detailing convoluted details. From my experience, sadly many businesses, enterprise, and transformation architects were frowned upon and told off when they delve into unnecessary architectural, business, design, specification, and other technical details when conversing with senior transformation executives.

Governance Simplicity for Digital Transformation

Creating and maintaining simplicity for the governance of digital transformation initiatives are critical success factors. To re-iterate the situation due to its criticality, complex and complicated governance processes and procedures can be obstacles for digital transformation initiatives. More precisely, these complex governance processes and procedures can cause delays, confusions, rework, and consequently, low performance for the digital transformation goals.

Because of these well documented and known implications, we must find novel ways to simplify governance framework, process, and procedures for digital transformation initiatives. We must be aware of the importance of governance and pay special attention to the required rigour delicately balanced with flexibility and speed.

We cannot compromise the quality requirements in governing digital transformation initiatives. However, while having an architectural rigour, we also need to have a fine balance for delivering the message quickly in the simplest possible terms and making the processes for governance in the most effective ways in the program.

As business architects and digital transformation governance leaders, we must stay on top of digital trends and developments to govern them for business transformation goals. As part of our architectural governance role in the program, we must ensure all technology practices adhere to regulatory standards in our business organisation's industries. Let's keep in mind that there may be varying industry regulation requirements in different business organisations.

Data Simplicity for Digital Transformation

Simplifying data, data platforms, and data practices is a widely discussed topic in digital transformation programs. There are several ways of simplifying data, data platforms, and data practices. One way of simplifying data is to clean it, remove duplications and errors, and bring it to a transformed state for consumption. From data platforms and practices perspectives, reducing data sources, data velocity, and data volumes, as needed, can also be considered to simplify and streamline data management processes for digital transformation initiatives.

However, there is a paradoxical situation to point out for data volumes and velocity as far as simplicity is concerned for digital transformation initiatives. For example, in general, the use of more datasets is believed to create complexity; however, this may not necessarily be true. It can be just the opposite situation for digitally transforming environments. Since we ingest more and richer data sources to feed the business systems and applications, the systems and applications can produce better output with increased quantities of data sets and data velocity. Of course, this situation requires substantial analysis, evaluation, and decision-making case by case conducted by data management experts in the digital transformation programs. I only highlighted this paradoxical point for business architects to challenge the common perceptions and misconceptions in the digital transformation programs which may occur from time to time.

We can achieve data simplicity through the right data analysis, intelligence, powerful tools, and effective management strategies. In other words, when correctly and purposefully analysed, more data can add better intelligence for modernising and transforming the data platforms for business insights.

We need to understand the importance of data for transformation initiatives and use established techniques and evolving methods in data science including machine learning. We can leverage industry knowledge and focus on simplifying data collection, process, management, storage, and analytics.

Besides, for enterprise modernisation and digital transformation purposes, the traditional data management methods cannot suffice; therefore, we need to consider Big Data management technologies, process, and tools to create and maintain simplicity.

One of the simplified Big Data trends in massive digital transformation and modernisation initiatives is the use of Cloud services for Big Data solutions. There is even a specific Big Data as a Service model that we can consider in our specific workload transformation goals. The next point in our simplification list is the presentation.

Presentation Simplicity

Business architects conduct substantial presentations to many stakeholders in the digital transformation program. We may need to provide many presentations to different stakeholders for enterprise digital transformation initiatives. We present to multiple groups using PowerPoint slides or Visio images. We need to use these tools very carefully to maintain the focus of the audience and effectively convey critical business messages. We must simplify our presentations for the effectiveness of our message to stakeholders, extended teams, and broader communities within the program.

'Dead from PowerPoint' is a famous statement depicting inefficiencies of presentations using an excessive number of slides and refers to just reading the points from the slides. Being brief and concise in presentations is also an essential simplification method for effective communication.

For example, we can simplify team presentations by cutting unnecessary, irrelevant details and using a concise number of slides focusing on necessary points when using a PowerPoint as a tool. The core message must be kept in mind at all times when presenting to relevant stakeholders.

Another crucial consideration is focusing on conveying the intended central message rather than trying to impress the audience with sophisticated communication techniques. Endless discussions may cloud the essential message; therefore, it is critical to control the presentation process and focus sharply on the essential points in our presentations.

We can provide simplified, clear, and concise presentations without compromising the quality of content and effectiveness of the message. We also can encourage the team members to follow simplicity principles in our presentations and provide constant constructive feedback to maintain this simplicity culture.

Chapter 4: Cost Considerations of Digital Transformation by Business Architecture

Purpose

The purpose of this chapter is to provide a high-level view of cost and business value propositions for digital transformation. Understanding the financial aspects of business architecture within digital transformation context can make valuable contributions to our program goals.

Arguably, for a business organisation, the financial aspect of digital transformation initiatives can be the most important one. Even if we create a paragon of architecture with flawless designs and specifications, if the proposed business architecture is economically not viable for the digital transformation program and it does not produce a compelling return on investment, it cannot be considered as successful.

Therefore, the financial focus for digital transformation becomes critical and must be a priority objective and key consideration in developing our business architecture. We need to consider the cost impact for every aspect and building blocks of the business architecture framework. A pragmatic business architectural approach with business priority focus is essential to keep the cost under control.

Cost Awareness for Digital Transformation

Every activity in digital transformation initiatives generates a substantial cost for business organisations. There are known and hidden costs. It is relatively more comfortable to deal with the known costs; we can apply some logic and resources to address them. However, the real challenge is to deal with the hidden costs.

Hidden costs are the more significant part of the proverbial iceberg. When we are developing cost cases and models for our digital transformation initiatives, we always need to challenge the norms especially capital expenditure which is traditionally used in many organisations. For example, infrastructure costs for a simple digital business development workload can be prohibitive; therefore, we may consider moving these low priority, less sensitive workloads to inexpensive public cloud service offerings. This can be pointed out in the capability's domain of the business architecture framework.

Even though financial teams manage the cost, the business architecture team need to find ways to make digital solutions inexpensive, affordable, and lowering the cost gradually without compromising quality. Quality considerations are the critical requirements of digital transformation initiatives. Therefore, quality aspect must be factored in the business architecture framework. Let's briefly touch on these concerns.

Quality and Cost Concerns

From various architecture and transformation communities, I witnessed a common perception of making digital transformation initiatives cost-effective without compromising quality. The reason behind this perception is that architects must make a considerable number of trade-offs. I partially agree with this statement.

As business architects in digital transformation programs, we can contribute to reducing the program costs by making trade-offs with a methodical and collaborative approach. For example, we can obtain collaborative input by bridging business and technology stakeholders. Our agile approach to our business architecture development and other innovative ways such as adding automation and standardisation to the program goals can make a real difference.

We can contribute to increasing the quality of the solutions by applying professional diligence, architectural rigour, agile delivery with iterative progress, smart collaboration across multiple business and technology teams, and harvesting re-usable materials for the program.

These principle-based and cost reduction approaches are necessary to maintain and even increase the desired quality in our digital transformation programs. Improving quality in a progressive way can have a favourable effect on the overall financial viability of digital transformation initiatives.

Bill of Materials for Digital Transformation

In some digital transformation programs, business architects are consulted or requested to help with creating Bill of Materials (BOMs) for the overall program. Simple yet a powerful impact on cost control can be related to providing effective BOMs in digital transformation programs.

Bill of Materials refers to hardware, software, licences, and services costs for the projects in a digital transformation program. As business architects, we can participate in the creation of cost case and cost model development proactively guiding through our business architecture framework and relevant architectural work-products, especially focussing on the business capability aspect of the organisation mapped to the program level. For example, we can provide guiding input for validating a BOM for a digital transformation project based on the business strategy that we set across the program and completed high-level architectural artefacts in the framework.

Regarding BOM approvals we must be very cautious because there may be tremendous pressure from project managers and procurement staff to generate an upfront BOM before architectural and design artefacts are approved. This is usually due to the urgent demands of the project delivery lifecycle for digital transformation initiatives. However, we can point out that without an approved business architecture, other architectural deliverables, and approved design artefacts, we cannot commence purchasing materials. The drawback is that most of the times, it is not possible to obtain refunds for that expensive equipment purchased upfront without proper architectural and design approvals.

This assertive and straightforward action from us and our team members can save a considerable amount of funds to the digital transformation program or save wasting tight budgets in this economic climate.

Unfortunately, I witnessed on several occasions, millions of dollars of materials purchased upfront and wasted due to changes in business, enterprise, and solution architectures, and detailed designs. These BOMs did not fit the purpose after all. This lesson learnt worth consideration.

Infrastructure & Maintenance Costs for Digital Transformation

There can be extensive infrastructure and maintenance costs in digital transformation programs associated with underlying infrastructure such as large data centres, server farms, mobile devices, storage units, data processing tools, analytics machines, and hosting in multi-Clouds.

These foundational infrastructure components are essential to make digital transformation initiatives viable. When we are developing our cost models after the approval of the business architecture framework, we ensure that business strategy and capability align with capital expenditure goals at the program level. There may be times that we can reuse some infrastructure components and tools across multiple projects in the digital transformation program. It can be useful for trying to procure internally first. This is a principle I developed in my extended teams, and we saved substantial amounts of funds in our digital transformation programs. As a side note, reusability is also environmentally friendly.

Another key consideration is a single point of failure in digital transformation solutions which may have a tremendous effect on the overall cost for the program. Single failure or defect in a device or a group of devices serving the consumers via these high-end technology stacks can adversely affect the service levels hence could lead to high costs for the service providers. As business architects who understand the business value, capability, and strategy, we can guide the domain and solution architects in the digital transformation programs to be aware of these high impact risks and voice our concerns in relevant governance forums across the program.

Availability and Performance Costs

Availability and performance of the systems are the significant factors to address punitive service levels for digital transformation programs. One way of addressing these risks is the introduction of automation to service management. As business architects, we can add this to the program action plan, introducing automation as a business capability, guiding solution architects, technical specialists, and other team members.

Automated SLAs for business can detect low availability and poor performance. These automated SLAs trigger the rules and force the business organisations breaching the agreements pay the contractually agreed penalties.

The service downtime is a critical factor and situation causing excessive penalties for the business organisation. The longer the systems are down, the higher the penalties can be. We need to take every measure from an architectural standpoint to minimise system downtimes.

As business architects, our contribution to availability and performance by taking necessary measures such improving the quality of architectural artefacts, especially by being a bridge between the business and architecture team, can make a substantial difference in cost management of digital transformation programs. We discuss the implications of SLAs in the next section.

Service Level Agreements

Service downtime costs can be very high based on agreed rates and cause excessive penalties when accumulated for service-level breaches by our business organisations. Service Level breaches also have a strategic adverse effect on an organisation's product, services, and overall business performance.

For example, downtimes in business services or defects in products can result in poor client satisfaction. If we also look at from the consumer perspectives, they lose business due to service downtimes. It is a lose-lose scenario even though the consumer organisations are compensated with SLA penalties paid by the service providers.

As business architects, we need to pay attention to the SLAs from the nascent stages of the digital solution lifecycle, starting from the business architecture framework phase. The higher the quality of the architectural guiding principles, the easier it can be for SLAs to meet when the digital transformation solutions are in production and the operational state. The rigour for quality in each phase can positively contribute to deal with SLA risks.

We can advise the solution architects that some of the key considerations to address SLA issues could be autonomous condition monitoring and remote maintenance for the devices or systems in remote locations. For example, sending a technician to a remote location may take several hours of travel. However, fixing those units can be done remotely in minutes. One simple yet powerful example in our projects that we applied was rebooting servers remotely. This simple task saved us a considerable amount of time and money. It also helped us prevent

SLA penalties associated with digital transformation projects as part of the program.

There are specialist solutions regarding these trending techniques. It can be useful to recommend and assign automation and standardisation specialists for the design of these unique features in our digital transformation programs.

Service level management is particularly crucial in digital initiatives. Let's put this into a practical perspective. One of the biggest fears of the business executives is the adverse impact of poor performance and availability problems damaging their client satisfaction and compromising business revenues in their transformed product and services.

To address the business risks associated with this valid business concern, as business architects we need to pay special attention to SLA strategy, planning, design, and implementation in an integrated way in our overall business architecture framework. A proactive and effective SLA management is one of the key areas where digital intelligence of business architects makes a real difference in cost management.

Digital Transformation Systems

Digital transformation programs are long journeys moving the core aspects of the business organisation from chaos to coherence. The transformation process includes many aspects of the core business systems. For the scope of this book, we focus on digital systems. Even though digital systems look only a tiny bit of a business organisation in overarching enterprise, this domain by itself can be gigantic, especially for core business units of the large organisations.

Digital systems in a business organisation can include business IT processes, business data, business applications, IT infrastructure, and IT service delivery. These domains can even be more complicated with the addition of geographical factors such as adding multiple countries to the equation.

One of the essential workaround solutions for dealing with this complexity is to modernise these primary domains iteratively in parallel. Let's review the methodical approach that I present in the next section.

Methodical Approach to Cost Management

As business architects leading and focussing on successful progress of a digital transformation program, we must follow a proven methodical approach to manage the cost and contribute to the business solution viability and profitability. Both a top-down and bottom-up approach must be applied depending on the needs.

At the top tier, we see the business and IT processes, and at the bottom tier, we see IT infrastructure. These two domains can independently be transformed using parallel activities. However, an integrated approach is essential as there can always be dependencies from multiple angles in both top-down and bottom-up approaches. As business architects, we must closely work with multiple domain architects, solution architects, and infrastructure architects across the program.

Once an organisation has an approved transformation strategy, then we can refine the strategy and convert it to clear architectural and technical formats. The strategy document is a critical artefact to bring all parties and stakeholders on the same page. Then we can identify the critical dependencies among these domains based on the short term, midterm, and long-term considerations.

By using the strategy and considering the dependencies, we need to develop a high-level roadmap to inform the sponsoring executives. This roadmap can indicate the key outcomes, timelines, and a ballpark cost for the overall modernisation and digital transformation activities. These indications initially can be at a very high level as there may be many factors affecting timelines, resources, and associated cost.

Once the roadmap for the digital transformation is set, we need to make a comprehensive viability assessment considering the current state of the scoped initiatives, their indicative future state, and the strategies to reach the end state. This viability assessment must include key risks, constraints, and dependencies. The viability assessment can be the most informative tool a lead business architect can provide to the sponsoring executives of the digital transformation program for them to make informed decisions leading to successful outcomes.

After review and approval of the viability assessment, we delve into collecting the high-level requirements of the initiative based on the domains we mentioned earlier. As dealing with the requirements of those domains can be daunting, we can delegate the requirements collection process with the domain, program, and solution architects, technical specialists, and business analysts based on their skills set relevant to the types of requirements.

In this phase, the role of the business architect is to coordinate and facilitate the requirements management team, which can consist of multiple solution architects, technical specialists, and business analysts.

After requirements are collected and analysed at a reasonable amount, the next important activity is to prioritise the requirements based on business impact. We need to develop criteria to prioritise the requirements based on factors depicted in the strategy and business roadmap documents, as well as the financial and business priorities set by the sponsoring executives.

Following this methodical yet straightforward approach, we can be on top of issues and contribute to the control of cost. Reducing cost can also increase the financial viability of the digital transformation initiative.

Besides we need to introduce a new way of thinking, continuous innovation, as a cost reduction enabler, as it can be the dominant player for overall cost management in complex digital environments. We cover the innovation in a separate chapter subsequently due to its significance in cost management and return on investment.

Chapter 5: Business Architecture Innovation & Invention Focus

Purpose

In this chapter, I attempt to reflect upon my observations and thoughts on how business architects can use innovative and inventive approach coupled with collaborative principles of fusion-focused approach to initiate, lead, empower digital transformation goals.

In this chapter, we aim to understand the importance of innovative and inventive approaches as an empowering factor for the success of digital transformation programs.

Let's have a common understanding of the innovative and inventive thinking process in this practical context. The subsequent sections lay out the key points.

Innovation and Invention

We can define innovative and inventive thinking in different terms based on the type of work, professions, industry, and other backgrounds relate to our digital transformation goals.

In this book, my definition of innovative and inventive thinking is the use of creativity for generating novel ideas, new methods, new approaches, new techniques, new processes, and new tools, or approaches to improve the current environment to gain insights, add compelling business value, reduce unnecessary costs, and increase desired revenue by focussing on return on investment which can incur from our digital transformation investments.

Innovation and invention relate to novelty, improvement, and iterations for ongoing steady progress. Innovative and inventive thinking generates novel ideas, focuses on improving ideas, and strives for making continuous iterative progress. To this end, this type of thinking can use agile delivery principles to reach our goals. Innovative and inventive thinking must be practical rather than theoretical hence they need to add immediate value.

Innovative and inventive thinking feeds the culture and is a critical aspect of a modernising ecosystem in transforming organisations for our digital transformation goals. Business cultures embracing innovative and inventive thinking approaches can naturally renew themselves to survive and thrive in fluctuating conditions, which are typical situations in modernising and transforming businesses. These business organisations can extend to the next generations with constant progress, renewed image, improved services, and stronger capabilities.

Innovation, inventions, excellence, and agility are interrelated and go hand in hand to produce successful outcomes. For example, innovative and inventive thinking ignites technical excellence, and technical excellence can be empowered by agility. Therefore, as business architects leading digital transformation programs, we must be natural innovators and inventors producing results with agility. These attributes are the critical success factors for our digital transformation programs.

We can practice innovative and inventive thinking in the program, turn it to daily habits, and motivate people around us. Now, let's attempt to find some practical ways to generate inventive and innovative intelligence to support our digital transformation goals.

Thinking Modes

Innovation and invention require multiple modes of thinking differently. Traditionally, most of us think vertically, linearly or in binary. We usually use vertical and linear types of thinking for problem-solving.

Linear thinking goes deep down, layer by layer, and in a sequential, and logical manner. Applying practical logic coupled with an agile approach streamlining our thoughts aligned with transformation goals are some useful approaches in this type of thinking mode.

There are times we may need to use binary thinking to assess and validate some immediate situations. Binary thinking consists of simple terms such as yes or no, black and white, good or bad. This type of thinking can be useful in a particular context however it has its limitations for qualitative assessment requirements.

As opposed to vertical thinking, horizontal thinking covers more breadth rather than depth and aims to generate unpredictable ideas by breaking out the rigid thought patterns. By using horizontal thinking in transformation activities, we challenge the assumptions posed in traditional situations. In this type of thinking mode, we look for alternatives and go beyond the ordinary. Horizontal thinking can lead to radically creative solutions.

We can apply horizontal thinking to transformation activities to create innovative and inventive ideas. There are various techniques that we can leverage horizontal thinking in our day to day activities.

Some commonly used techniques for horizontal thinking are randomisations, distortions, reversals, exaggerations, metaphors, analogies, dreaming, theme mining, questioning the norms, and creating contradictions. Using these techniques opens new opportunities for our creativity.

Another practical technique to generate innovative and inventive ideas is to use mind mapping practice. Using mind maps, we can articulate our thoughts with representative maps on a paper or a whiteboard.

We can also use other visual representations, such as drawing pictures on a whiteboard while explaining abstract ideas. We can visualise abstract ideas better by looking at the drawing as the proverbial a single picture can tell a thousand words. As business architects, our thinking mode makes a substantial difference in demonstrating our leadership in digital transformation programs.

Creating Innovation and Invention Culture

Many digitally transforming business organisations attempt to create desirable innovation and invention cultures supporting the transforming digital ecosystems. As business architects, we are the catalyst for the formation and maintenance of this type of empowering culture.

With the support of the technical team members in our digitally transforming ecosystem, we continually challenge the status quo. Our team members tend to embrace changes and challenges by seeing the transformation at first hand in these cultures.

People collaborate better in cultures embracing innovative and inventive ideas. They see themselves in new positions with positively changing conditions. They do not resist change as they know that change can be useful for them.

In these enriching cultures, business organisations create excellence centres or ideation labs for people to try new ideas. These empowered employees perform ongoing trials and errors to create and test compelling ideas leading to new business capabilities and revenue streams. These highly motivated employees may fail at times, but they fail quickly and come back to reality with improved knowledge. They start seeing the failed tests as new definitions.

Harnessing and driving creative thinking may result in new and enriched cultures. As business architects, we need to cultivate the transforming culture and inspire our team members. The best way to ignite innovation and invention for inspiration is to be a role model for our team members. We need to encourage the team members to innovate, invent, and reward them for their achievements.

In transforming organisations, innovation and invention become habitual. Our team members can strive for excellence by creating new ideas in their day to day tasks. The culture dictates that no one should be called with weird names or with other judgemental adjectives. Instead, new ideas are welcomed, praised, and even awarded in different ways.

In our transforming environments, our team members embrace constant change and new ideas, even if these challenges can be painful at times. We learn how to turn the pain to pleasure with the rewarding results of evident transformations.

Metaphorically, innovation is like air and water for our survival. In addition to survival, we need to use innovative and inventive thinking for thriving. We not only need to create innovations and inventions at a personal level but also through collaboration with the immediate teams and extended teams.

In our transforming environments, we must keep asking how to deliver innovative and inventive experiences moment by moment continuously. This is a cultural shift that we all need to embrace collective success.

Design Thinking for Digital Transformation

One of the recent powerful methods we can use to maintain an innovative and inventive culture can be achieved by the use of the design thinking practice in the digital transformation programs. This can take place daily in the team interactions in the digital transformation programs.

Design thinking can empower the team to be intuitive and logical at the same time. Design thinking enables team members to be more creative to recognise new patterns in transforming environments. We can apply design thinking principles to our digital transformation activities at all times. Because, design thinking practice makes us empathetic to our business users and to their needs.

As design thinking is closely associated with the agile approach, the design thinking professionals progress their ideas iteratively. Digital transformation initiatives require the adoption of design thinking to their core culture. Design thinking can result in a creative cultural shift to support our digital transformation goals.

Growth Mindset for Digital Transformation

As business architects, we must have a growth mindset to ignite innovation and invention in our digital transformation programs. We can get our team members with a fixed mindset to convert to a growth mindset.

It is evident that a growth mindset can lead to innovative and inventive solutions; it must be a build-in characteristic in the personalities of people in the transforming ecosystem.

As business architects, not only we have it, but also, we must lead to a mindset shift in immediate and extended teams. We must hold a positive 'can do' attitude for any challenges we come across in our digital transformation programs.

By demonstrating a growth mindset, we can have a customer-centric mindset and put ourselves in customers' shoes with strong empathy. Applying design thinking techniques, we can develop empathy maps which can enable us to think like our customers. The growth mindset based on empathy is part of the design thinking practice and can be embedded in our transformation culture.

Co-creation for Digital Transformation

To ignite innovation and invention culture in digital transformation programs, we must consider market conditions and the needs of our clients. These challenging conditions can help us generate new ideas. Listening to our clients carefully and collaborating with them can help us focus on innovative thinking and enable us to invent novel solutions.

Many innovations and inventions can be co-created with clients. Co-creation can be seen as a win-win situation for both the service providers and their consumers.

A client-centric innovation and invention approach can be invaluable for digital transformation goals. We can link client concerns, business capabilities, business requirements, expectations, and aspirations to our organisation's business capabilities then define the focus areas for innovation and invention agendas to enable our digital transformation goals to address client needs.

Innovation and Invention Roadblocks

There can be many visible and invisible roadblocks to creating innovation and inventions in digital transformation programs; therefore, it is critical for us to recognise the potential roadblocks.

The roadblocks can be in different shapes and forms from various angles. For example, one of the main roadblocks can be keeping the status quo and silos in traditional business organisations. These organisations and their business processes usually tend to maintain the status quo isolated from other entities of the business. They continue operating in silos. There may be strong resistance to change and amalgamation in traditional business cultures.

Many business organisations nowadays recognise the importance of innovative and inventive thinking to achieve digital transformation goals. However, there may be unknown fears and resistance towards novelties by some team members who may have hidden or differing agendas to the core values of the business. These variances in team goals may constitute political, economic, commercial and cultural implications.

As business architects, it is our duty to be alert and recognise team members who may have different agendas and intentionally or unintentionally try to sabotage innovative and inventive thinking in our transformation goals. Even though these colleagues with a negative mindset may be in the minority, they still can have a tremendous adverse impact on desired progress.

One way of dealing with these difficult people is to be transparent to them and have a close face to face conversations explaining our common goals and the benefits they may gain. We can find ways to engage those types of team members and show the value and benefit of new ideas which can benefit them. If those people can see the value for themselves, then they can be converted to our supporters of digital transformation goals. The critical point is engaging them and encouraging them to think positively.

The business as a usual mentality in the traditional business organisations can be a roadblock for infusing new ideas. Our team members dealing with the business as usual aspects all the time create a comfort zone manifested as habitual behaviour. The constantly changing transformation activities can be seen as disruptors of their comfort zones. More importantly, tired employees can hardly have any interest in innovation and inventions as they cannot see the immediate benefit.

One of the workaround solutions for dealing with comfort zone issues can be to separate new and old business as usual teams in two different departments. However, we must find some collaborative ways to bridge them to maintain productivity.

Of course, business, as usual, is essential for business organisations to continue their current functions but these organisations also need innovation and invention for transforming to the digital world with new insights, market competitiveness, and new revenue generation.

It is usually a good idea that the digital transformation programs can be kept separate from the business as usual practices to prevent any adverse effect of traditional thinking; however, we must integrate them in a way to prevent the undesirable effects of the old thinking models.

In traditional business organisations, we also need to watch out cumbersome business processes which can be deterrent factors for innovation and invention goals for transformation. Activities may take too long to complete, and the team members struggle to cope with the difficulties in dealing with archaic processes. We highlighted the importance of simplifying the processes in the previous chapter.

Chapter 6: Accelerated Business Outcomes for Digital Transformation

Purpose

Accelerating our business architecture delivery with using agile approach is the next critical pillar in our digital transformation method. As business architects, in this era, we must be nimble, agile and think on our feet at all times.

Approaching our goals with agility provides us with a competitive advantage in our business organisation and can help us to be influential, credible, competitive, and productive in our digital transformation engagements.

We need to be mindful that our business teams and customers expect us to act in agility. As business architects, we need to embrace agile architectural response and delivery and make it as part of our transforming culture. We need to delve into details on how to develop an agile culture to accelerate our digital transformation delivery. Let's start with agile thinking and acting.

Agile Thinking and Acting

In this day and age, agile thinking and acting are essential attributes for the business architects leading digital transformation programs. We cannot afford slow thinking and acting in this climate to respond effectively for rapidly changing business environments.

By using agile thinking and rapid actions, we can ask empowering questions by comparing, connecting, and contrasting at all times. For example, we keep asking how we can make our business and IT footprint more intuitive, responsive, and nimble day today while remaining a reliable business service offering.

This type of thinking mode is a foundational requirement of our modernisation and digital transformation initiatives. Whist dealing with legacy business and IT footprint to understand it in an agile manner, we also need to have the vision of well-functioning business solutions, profitable business capabilities, and put our energies on rapid-paced iterative digital transformation initiatives. Dealing with opposing situations may require a delicate balance.

It is not feasible to undertake successful digital transformation initiatives with an old way of thinking and using old methods. As this becomes a reality, many organisations embrace agile methods and mature in delivering rapidly.

We know that agility is a particular concern for digital transformation programs as consumer demands are increasing based on fast-paced delivery requirements. To meet the challenges of these rapid changes and growing demands, we need to apply agile thinking and acting to our digital transformation pursuits. Let's touch the importance of speed for market advantage.

Speed to Market

Speed to market for any contemporary business organisation is one of the most fundamental requirements of digital transformation initiatives. We can generate revenues for our business organisations only by acting very quickly in this competitive world.

To this end, fast delivery using agile approaches became the new norm in transforming enterprises. Our business products are expected to be released faster than they were in the past. For example, security updates and bug fixes for business applications are required more frequently.

Speed to market affects all aspects of digitally transforming business organisations and creates many challenges for business service providers. These challenges make it imperative to act, behave, and approach in agility to stay competitive in the market.

Promoting Accelerated Delivery

Accelerated delivery is essential to achieve our digital transformation goals. However, there may be some resistance to accelerated approaches in some traditionally slow-acting business organisations.

The good news is that promoting accelerated delivery to many business stakeholders nowadays can be reasonably easy due to its benefits and compelling business value in the competitive marketplace.

As a positive aspect, accelerated delivery is a particular interest to new generations as they grow with agility in all walks of life. However, the older generation still has a sentimental attachment to traditional approaches, for example, they are adamant for using waterfall methods to achieve their business goals.

There appears to be some comfort zone created for using waterfall methods in traditional business organisations. Therefore, we need to be influential and find some creative ways and demonstrate compelling benefits to promote agile approaches to those resisting them; particularly to older generations.

Quality Perceptions for Fast Delivery

There is a common perception that fast delivery methods such as agile approach can cut things short hence may reduce the quality outcome that business strives for; however, this is not necessarily true. Digital transformation programs applying agile approaches can increase the quality with the progressive and iterative approaches by checking quality more frequently in every iteration and milestone.

We must articulate the benefits and compelling reasons to use the agile approach, especially for digital transformation goals. It is not advisable to wait and see the end of a gigantic digital transformation program. There are always many unknowns; hence, it is not possible to see the end business product without experimentation and constant trial and errors in smaller scales.

An accelerated business delivery method using an agile approach allows the team members to test their ideas quickly and iteratively. If they fail, they fail quickly and cheaply without costing lots of funds to the initiatives.

The business value gained by accelerated delivery methods needs to be understood well and needs to be embedded in the culture of the organisations striving for digital transformation goals. As business architects, we can be the catalyst for conveying the message and making the necessary cultural adjustments effectively in our architecting teams.

As business architects, we must be motivators and ignite accelerated delivery in our digital transformation initiatives. As we are business-focused and technically capable at the architectural level, we can show the business value and share our knowledge and views with our technical team members and business stakeholders.

As a role model business architects, we can provide ongoing feedback and architectural support to the scrum teams striving for accelerated delivery using agile approaches. Business architects must be agile champions to accelerate architectural delivery for digital transformation goals in the program.

Roles and Responsibilities for Accelerated Delivery

Accelerated delivery for digital transformations requires multiple roles and responsibilities. An accelerated delivery approach requires using an agile method across multiple teams called scrum teams. These teams work collaboratively, closely, and in an integrated way.

The most common roles in agile teams are the scrum master, the product owner, and the scrum team members. As business architects, we can perform the role of the product owner for digital transformation programs representing the business. As we are architecting the digital solutions from a business perspective, we are in an excellent position to own the digital product or services that we are architecting.

As product owners, we can set the acceptance criteria for a digital business product or service in the allocated transformation sprint. Providing a practical acceptance criterion can lead the team to think in the right direction. Our leadership and ownership of digital business products are paramount for the success of accelerated delivery in the digital transformation programs.

Sometimes, we can also serve as a scrum master in a digital transformation program. The scrum master role requires us to provide day to day guidance on developing agile user stories, clearing backlogs, running stand-up meetings, and designing iterative business solutions for digital transformation initiatives. This is a lead architecting role for the accelerated business services delivery.

Agile Awareness for Accelerated Delivery

Agile awareness for digital transformation initiatives requires developing quick mental models on how business and technology users interact with the services in each iteration. To maintain accelerated delivery, we need to apply agile principles. For example, using these agile principles, we can clear our transformation backlogs in the most efficient ways. Clearing our backlogs rapidly and efficiently is essential for accelerated delivery.

To deliver with speed, we need to prioritise our business architectural backlogs within various initiatives of the digital transformation program. With our rapid action-oriented approach, we can clear the backlogs quickly in priority orders. Furthermore, we can use rewards and recognise the high achievers' effort and contributions for clearing the backlogs in the most effective and innovative ways.

In many organisations, due to valid reasons, developing business and technical architecture and convoluted designs can create fear for the sponsors. The main reason for this is that architecture involves things that are hard to change later and imminently cost them substantial funds.

However, this doesn't mean we cannot apply an accelerated approach to business architecture. Our awareness of accelerated delivery and applying it at a constant basis can add significant value to complete our business, architectural, and design activities.

There is a massive trend to use accelerated delivery methods for developing architectural and design activities for digital transformation initiatives.

To address the fear of architecture and designs, I introduce the term pragmatic business architecture in fast-paced modernisations and digital transformation initiatives in my recent projects. Let's discuss the importance and necessity of using a pragmatic architecture approach.

Pragmatic Architecture Approach

We know that predicting the future is very hard; almost impossible. Therefore, creating an upfront paragon of business architecture is not practical. To this end, as business architects, we must take a pragmatic approach to architecture development when engaged in leading digital transformation programs.

Pragmatism negates perfectionism. The notion of perfection equates to failure in fast-paced digital transformation programs. We cannot afford the use of monolithic waterfall methods for perfecting and developing business architecture frameworks and designs for many months and even years. This slow approach is not sustainable and does not suit the demands of digital transformation goals.

Taking extended times for creating business architecture frameworks is not feasible in this fast-paced digital age anymore. Consumers expect business product and services much quicker than old times. Our business profitability depends on our speed to market. Therefore, a pragmatic and accelerated approach to business architecture and design artefacts is essential for successful digital transformation initiatives.

To enable accelerated delivery for architecting, an iterative business approach to architecture can be the most effective investment in the earlier stages of the digital transformation. We can see business architecture development like product development. The incremental and iterative approach can speed up the architectural process and improve the quality of architecting based on the minimally viable product development approach.

Another way of accelerated pragmatic approach is to use a single business domain and apply the learnings to the next domains. This single business domain approach allows us to progress incrementally with an iterative approach. This approach can help us progress with confidence depicting a well-managed risk profile.

Accelerated Development

After business architecture and technical design, another big topic and concern in digital transformation initiatives are software or application development.

Development activities are time-consuming and can be very costly. We are not developers, but we guide the developers and create a bridge between business and the development team. Therefore, we need to understand the new trends that the business needs from the development teams.

For example, as we all know, by using traditional waterfall approaches developing a software product used to take months and years in the past. Nowadays, our consumers cannot wait this long anymore. The solution to accelerated development phase is applying an agile approach to software development. Fortunately, agile methods are more suited to the development areas and broadly accepted by modern developers. As business architects, we can advise the use of agile to the development process and factor it in our business architecture framework.

There are many evolving agile methods to support different kinds of software and application development processes. Fortunately, many software and application developers understand the importance of agile methods and embrace them. These developers can see the results much more quickly by accelerating the delivery for consumer and market demands.

As business architects we can recommend the use of evolving methods such as DevOps as prime considerations for accelerating delivery of software and application development initiatives for digital transformation programs. DevOps brings the software development and infrastructure support operations teams together in an integrated way. The developers don't have to concern about the infrastructure issues anymore. Applying DevOps practice to digital transformation initiatives can speed up the delivery of software products for timely consumption.

As business architects, we can encourage rapid application development and deployment of flexible solutions using appropriate agile methods and DevOps principles in our digital transformation programs.

We need to be mindful that speedy time-to-market for digital products and services is a competitive differentiator in this day and age. The rapid application and software development solutions for business market demands can also delight our clients and increase their confidence in our business products and services.

Accelerate Delivery with Automation and Standardisation

Enterprise modernisation goals leading to digital transformation for our services and delivering our products fast to market requires substantial automation and standardisation activities. We can advise leveraging the benefits of automation and standardisation for accelerated delivery.

Principally, agile methods have a particular focus on automation and standardisation hence mandate applying them as much as possible in every scrum. It is well known that both automation and standardisation can enable simplifying and speeding up processes to meet consumer demands for digital services.

As we understand the value of process automation and standardisation for increasing the quality of our business products and services, we need to encourage our teams to leverage these two enablers in our digital transformation services. Many teams would embrace both automation and standardisation as the value is quite clear and compelling.

Applying process automation and standardisation to our digital transformation objectives, we can reduce the number of resources required to maintain manual and tedious tasks. As a matter of fact, computers and robotics can manage repetitive tasks much more effectively than human beings.

Process automation and standardisation can address human errors and resolve potential errors quickly. Business organisations embracing accelerated delivery and agile cultures do not resist automation and standardisation; in fact, they leverage these critical capabilities for the success of their digital transformation goals.

As business architects, by encouraging our domain architects, solutions designers, subject matter experts, and technical specialists to automate and standardise the tedious processes as much as possible, we can enable these valuable resources to participate in more value-adding roles rather than performing repetitive and boring tasks that computers and simple robots can undertake.

Team members focusing on stimulating and high-value items also tend to create more innovative solutions to empower digital transformation progress.

Accelerate Delivery by Breaking Silos

Accelerated delivery for digital transformations requires removing silos in business organisations. What I mean by silos are having isolated departments and teams without being integrated into other relevant departments and teams in the organisation. This undesirable separation is unnecessary and can be unproductive.

Silos in business organisations are proven to slow the whole digital transformation lifecycle, including business architecture, technical design, application development, solution deployment, marketing, and selling products and services.

Siloed cultures can also impact the quality of the products due to a lack of integrated views. Business departments in silos may not know each other's progress and cause some duplicate of works or rework. They may not produce a single integrated product or services to the consumers and delay the delivery pace.

Another undesirable implication of having silos in business organisations is that some departments in these traditional settings in the same organisations even compete with each other. Internal competition is the worst enemy which can slow down and destroy any digital transformation goals and objectives.

Leveraging our accelerated delivery mindset, we can move from silos to a flatter structure to resolve the issues of isolated and hierarchical structures in large organisations. By leveraging the agile principles, we can pay special attention to collaboration, co-locations, and face to face teamwork rather than having silos and hierarchies in our business organisations, leading to faster delivery for digital transformation product and services.

Maintaining an accelerated delivery mindset, we continuously need to deal with an aging culture to prevent it to the speedy delivery of our digital transformation goals. In short, we need to break silos for accelerated delivery. Instead of coming above, we can create flat structures, resulting in collaborative self-managing teams with many business domain experts as peers for accelerated delivery.

Accelerate Delivery by Prioritising Backlogs

Inevitably, digital transformation initiatives can have gigantic backlogs. Dealing with accumulated digital transformation backlogs can be daunting and discouraging for accelerated delivery.

However, our agile awareness mandating prioritisation can serve well in clearing backlogs efficiently and rapidly. Maintaining backlogs in agile methods is systemic and embedded in the culture. As business architects in scrums, we can make day to day management of backlogs in priority order, a habit.

Even if we perform the role of a scrum master or a product owner, we need to keep the team members accountable for their backlog items. We can help the team manage their assigned backlogs items in priority order effectively.

We cannot emphasise enough that as business architects, we must focus on the priority items in the digital transformation backlogs based on precise priority orders set by our digital transformation strategy and aligned with our accelerated delivery vision, goals, and objectives.

Leveraging this priority approach day to day and encouraging our team members to do so, our transformation backlogs can run efficiently and productively. We know that backlog management is a critical factor for accelerated delivery of our digital transformation sprints. We keep sprinting with prioritised acceleration.

Accelerate Delivery with Minimum Viable Product

One of the critical aspects of accelerated delivery is the creation of a minimum viable product using agile principles. We practice this acceleration using the well-recognised sprint concept as part of the agile scrum process.

A sprint is the shortest time bombed duration to create the minimum viable product. A sprint duration usually is a two to three-week period. This limited-time pressure facilitates to speed up delivery and encourages the team to focus on the priority items to create the minimum viable product in the digital transformation program.

In general, consumer expectations, financial constraints, resource issues, and business priorities can have an impact on setting priorities to clear our digital transformation initiative backlogs to create minimum viable products for the consumers of the program outputs.

This agile principle of creating a minimum viable product can help us set the priorities for business value creation for digital transformation goals aiming to delight our clients for accelerated delivery of our services progressively.

Accelerate Delivery with Constant Change

Accelerated delivery mandates dealing with constant change in business organisations. Change management is a vital aspect of digital transformation initiatives.

For the entire digital transformation team, embracing change is critical with accelerated delivery is a critical success factor. Quickly adapting to the constant change in the program can help us keep the momentum to create and maintain accelerated delivery.

Managing every user story in the sprint, clearing backlog items on a timely basis, and running a sprint efficiently is all about accelerated delivery with constant change in the program. Dealing with this constant change requires flexibility and agility in architecting, designing, developing, and implementing rapid business solutions for the customers.

To this end, business architects and the architecting team members engaged in the accelerated delivery processes of the program must adapt to the constant change. Our role as business architects requires to become the change agents in the digital transformation programs. The success of our digital transformation initiatives depends on change-oriented accelerated delivery.

Accelerate Delivery by Failing Rapidly, Early, and Cheaply

As we keep highlighting throughout this book, one of the benefits of using accelerated approach comes from progressing in small steps rapidly. In other words, we tackle problems and plans in smaller chunks in an accelerated mode.

Accelerated delivery empowered by an accepted agile approach in the program mandates the agile principles of the "fail fast, fail early, and fail cheaply". These principles are well proven in entrepreneurial settings hence can be seen as fundamental success factors for our digital transformation goals.

Of course, we don't just fail for the sake of failure. No one truly enjoys failure itself, however it can be beneficial to fail earlier than later to keep the cost of failure relatively low and turn the learnings to successful outcomes in the long run, particularly leveraging the lessons learnt from these smaller failures. Learning from failed attempts and redefining success is a crucial agile intelligence attribute for business architects and the architecting team members.

Even though we call it 'fail fast', realistically the term refers to ongoing experimentation with constant trial and errors leading to augmented intelligence and constantly learning to deal with unknowns in an accelerated, effective, and productive way.

Learnings from our iterative and incremental experimentations constitute desired progress for architecting, designing, developing, and implementing complex digital business transformation solutions.

Accelerated Business Cost Management

Accelerated delivery in a digital transformation program mandates business cost awareness. In business organisations, every resource and effort constitute a cost. The accelerated delivery approach can help us reduce business cost in various ways.

As applying accelerated delivery in our business architecture and technical design activities, we contribute to reducing the cost of delivery for our digital transformation initiatives. Business architects are expected to be cost-aware architects. We need to focus on how to reduce cost with our bridging capabilities, business capability understanding, and intelligent business and architectural decisions which may affect the overall digital transformation program.

By delivering rapidly and iteratively, we can make our business profitable, and contribute to generate more revenue. As mentioned previously, we can focus on increasing efficiencies via standardisation and automation, which consequently can lower traditional business costs as a response to our digital business transformation strategy.

To re-iterate, an accelerated delivery approach is a cost-focused and revenue-generating mechanism for the digital transformation programs. We can manage costs better and generate more revenue by adopting agile principles in high impact business-related tasks and technical solution development activities in our digital transformation programs.

Through incremental progress, prioritised backlog management, speedy iterative delivery through sprints, we can prevent the cost of failure for big chunks of work items and more importantly, we can turn the costs into revenues.

As business architects and architecting team members, we are expected and capable of turning costs to investment. With a strong vision, innovative approaches, and agile delivery capabilities, the costs incurred from our business initiatives can be perceived as an investment rather than cost.

Sponsoring executives of the digital transformation initiatives are aware that investment on visionary and well-performing digital business leaders like us, both at tactical and strategic levels, can help generate new business opportunities and can bring substantial revenues through the digital transformation initiatives.

Chapter 7: Collaboration of Business and Technology for Digital Transformation Initiatives

Purpose

As business architects and architecting team members, we certainly need to take leverage of collaborative intelligence across the business organisation and beyond to create a competitive advantage for our digital transformation pursuits.

In this section, our aim is to cover the importance of collaboration from a productivity angle reflected upon the digitally transforming business organisation. Let's understand the meaning and context of collaboration for our purpose.

Meaning of Collaboration

We know that the term collaboration is overused and sometimes loses its significance, especially with the emergence of internet technologies. People keep focusing on collaborative or collaboration tools, especially in a social media context.

In its true meaning, collaboration refers to a team of people working together for mutual goals to achieve successful and synergetic outcomes regardless of the medium. The team, mutual goals, and synergetic outcomes are essential entities of this simple framework. Our focus is, of course, on the work aspect of the collaboration rather than entertainment or hobbies.

Collaboration may take place in different modes and formats. One example is two or more people sharing ideas for a business project plan. At a basic level, people may also collaborate by writing using various documentation tools such as Box, Google docs, or network version of Microsoft Office products.

There are also emerging tools mainly used in mobile settings. These mobility tools are widespread in agile methods. To give an idea, some of these tools are Slack, Trello, Twitter, Facebook Messenger, and many more keep popping up every day.

Most of us tout social media tools as practical, useful, and highly valuable for collaboration purposes. However, when we carefully examine these tools, we can see that they are more information-sharing tools rather than actual collaboration tools. From my experience, the most productive and impactful collaboration tools are face to face meetings, good old phone, and interactive video conferencing.

Collaboration is essential to create synergy for digital transformation teams. As digital business architects, we are expected to collaborate widely and productively. We also motivate our team members to collaborate effectively and efficiently by pointing out the common goals and making them compelling for collaboration. Related to team collaboration, we need to understand the powerful metaphor of fusion within the transformation context.

Collaborative Insights with Fusion

We can consider fusion an empowering attribute for business architects and the architecting team members working in the digital transformation programs. The term fusion refers to joining different things with different attributes or functions together to create a single new entity or form. The notion of fusion relates to concepts such as integration, blending, merging, amalgamation, synergy, and bonding.

Fusion is closely related to collaboration from several angles. For example, the term fusion is a type of collaboration designed for specific and advanced missions. Fusion principles suit the goals of digital transformation progress in a business organisation.

Fusion principles aim to bring individual team members from various backgrounds, small groups with different purposes, various teams with differing capabilities, communities of practices with different missions under a single umbrella for serving a joint mission.

Fusion is the most advanced and effective type of collaboration especially required for complex and complicated digital transformation initiatives with unique goals and market focus. Creating fusion-based collaboration can be very challenging. As business architects, with extensive business, technical, and people skills, expertise, and experiences, we can create fusion-based collaboration for our digital transformation goals.

Besides, the term 'fusion' can also refer to integrating old systems, tools, and processes hence enabling to create new and synergetic entities. This transformative approach can be a critical success factor for our digital transformation goals. From an awareness perspective, we need to understand the significance of fusion principles and apply them to help our organisations to transform the business services and products to the digital goals effectively.

There are different ways to enable fusion in a business organisation. As business architects, we usually take responsibility to initiate fusion in our immediate and extended teams in the digital transformation programs.

Passion is required to achieve our digital goals using fusion principles. We don't wait for fusion to happen by itself. We know that nothing can happen by itself. Naturally, someone with leadership and architectural skills, like us, must initiate it. This action-oriented focus on fusion is one of the outstanding characteristics of strategic business architects, who are typically extrovert people.

Once we initiate fusion principles at the business architecture level and invite our collaborators to structured business and architectural activities within the program, then we can maintain necessary communication and engagement rules. Effective communication is a critical enabler of our fusion goals.

Depending on the medium, both verbal and written communication types can be required for fusion to happen.

Creating a fusion focus for co-located teams are usually conducted on face to face and can primarily be dynamic from a delivery perspective. However, geographically distant teams usually can use interactive video conferencing, telephone, chat programs, email, or various agile collaboration tools that we mentioned before.

Written communication can be a critical success factor for creating an effective fusion for remote teams. Written communication can cause some challenges. For example, a careless piece of writing may cause some offence and may kill the spirit of collaboration. Therefore, as business architects, we play an essential role in facilitating written communication by moderating communication channels delicately.

After we initiate and enable fusion goals across our teams, we need to keep the momentum going and sustain the desired outcomes. We take necessary measures and create the fundamental process and procedures to maintain collaborative activities across the teams. Effective use of our business and strategic leadership skills, as business architects, is essential to achieve fusion goals for the success of digital transformation initiatives.

Even though we set the initial team and processes to support the team activities, it is also the responsibilities of other team members to contribute to the goals set by our collaborative plans. To this end, as business architects, we also take the role of motivators to keep the digital transformation team inspired by showing our impactful vision and strategic goals.

By focusing on productive fusion at various levels, we can leverage insights from cross-functional teams and community of practices to create differentiating business value propositions for our digital transformation goals.

By undertaking many tasks to initiate and maintain fusion, we keep repeating these activities multiple times with multiple teams and integrate these teams to aggregate more intensive collaboration.

The magic of fusion in business organisations starts with ongoing repetitions. Successful repetitions can make ripple effects leading to more frequent success. In a relatively short time frame, these teams can create a collaborative culture based on fusion principles aligned with the business organisation's transforming ecosystem and strategic goals.

This collaborative culture in business organisations can be invaluable. When collaborative culture starts flourishing by using fusion-based collaboration, a desirable phenomenon called "innovation" happens naturally and keep flourishing.

Collaboration, fusion, and innovation are tightly coupled concepts and processes, as we mentioned in previous chapters. As a critical subject, it is necessary to discuss diversity within collaboration and fusion context.

Diversity for Digital Transformation

The power of connected people from diverse backgrounds for the same goal generates new ideas and insights within the digital transformation programs. Some of these ideas and insights may touch stakeholders coming from different angles and can further motivate them even to take more responsibilities in the digitally transforming business ecosystem.

With the ignition of the initial diversity focussed strategic leadership, this shift causes the emergence of new business and technical leaders in digitally transforming business environments.

Constant focus on innovation can generate collaborative culture and can be highly desirable for creating new business and growing established businesses by leading to desired digital transformation goals. Innovation is one of the exciting results provided by a collaborative culture with diversity, inclusiveness, and the implementation of a fusion approach.

Diversity oriented magical aspect of fusion and collaboration (leading to innovation) is an ideal situation for digitally transforming the business organisation. As business architects, we must take advantage of this desirable opportunity by creating, maintaining, facilitating, and further improving the situations in our digital transformation programs.

Collaborative Influence

Our business architecture, digital awareness, and people skills, as business architects and the architecting team, can help influence our extended team members to collaborate more effectively. Influence is an essential business and strategic leadership attribute in digital transformation initiatives.

Influence can be particularly essential to create a collaborative culture in transforming our legacy business environments. As business architects, and architecting team for digital transformation, our influence can make a substantial impact on moving towards transformed business environments.

As digital business architects, we must influence our collaborators by demonstrating responsibility, accountability, and credibility in our actions and behaviour. Due to its importance for business architects responsible for digital transformation, we need to discuss an important topic, 'credibility', in the next section.

Leadership Credibility for Digital Transformation

Credibility in dynamic business environments, such as in digital transformation teams, can be seen as a mandatory leadership attribute. More precisely, as business architects responsible for transforming environments, we must be credible for our business understanding and architectural leadership capabilities at all times.

Promoting change in our dynamic environments and obtaining buy-in for transforming from our business stakeholders and technical team members can require well-established leadership credibility.

As business architects, we can earn the trust of our collaborators by demonstrating our leadership credibility and integrity. Our business vision, architectural strategy, business understanding, skills, and constructive actions can have a tremendous impact on demonstrating our leadership credibility. Our architecting business goals and our organisations' business goals must align with these critical attributes.

Consistency and predictability for our behaviour and actions within our programs are critical success factors for demonstrating leadership credibility in these dynamic business environments. To survive, thrive, and succeed in our digital transformation goals, we must pay special attention to our professional behaviour and leadership actions to remain credible at all times in digitally transforming business environments.

Trust and Collaborative Engagement

When we establish trust with business stakeholders, architectural and technical teams, another magic can happen. These stakeholders and team members start sharing their true selves. They become more open, productive, and creative. Collaborative business culture is an empowering contributor and enabler of digitally transforming business organisations.

Digital transformation requires people from diverse background to engage in collaborative business activities. Enabling diversity is a critical success factor in creating collaborative business teams and an inclusive business culture in digitally transforming organisations.

Diversity is extra critical for digital transformation goals due to the required creativity and innovation by people from different backgrounds, skills sets, and experiences to realise the transformation goals.

We can establish diversity by demonstrating trust and integrity in our teams. It is essential to highlight that only with trust and in trusted environments, people can show their true identities. When people start showing their true selves, a diverse culture starts flourishing. Diversity is an enhancer of collaboration and fusion required for successful digital transformation initiatives.

More importantly, with diversity, also, innovation comes to the picture within the program. We can notice innovation growing stronger and faster. Diverse ideas can ignite and accelerate innovation. With this approach, we can create new options and choices in digital transformation programs.

Connecting those choices and options also can make a ripple effect on the business culture. With this understanding, we can conclude that integrity and trust-based diversity can be a valuable contributor to digital transformation programs.

Chapter 8: Leverage Emerging Technology & Tools for Digital Transformation

Purpose

As business architects, we need to find ways to leverage emerging technology and tools for digital transformation initiatives. In this chapter, our aim is to cover the prominent technologies and briefly introduce them by highlighting their importance for digital transformation goals.

Instead of delving into details and providing an exhaustive list, our focus is only on foundational technologies which can make a real difference for digital transformation initiatives. Let's touch on the critical technologies and technical skills that business architects and the architecting team need to possess for leading successful digital transformation initiatives.

In addition to business understanding, a broad technology awareness is a mandatory attribute for business architects to succeed in digital transformation programs. Our skills must be up-to-date with digital technologies and possess a wide range of vital technical knowledge to back up our business architecture capabilities.

There are many growing and emerging technologies that we need to be conversant. As business architects, we can encourage using emerging technologies as enablers of the digital transformation goals.

Enabling Technologies for Digital Transformation

The key technology enablers of digital business transformation goals are Cloud Computing, Mobile technologies, IoT, Big Data, and AI-based or Cognitive Data Analytics.

An integrated view of these technologies, associated processes, and tools are critical success factors in our digital endeavours.

In addition, we must be aware of the benchmarking of technological products and services as they are essential enablers of our digital business transformation initiatives. Let's start by introducing the relevance and importance of Cloud Computing.

Cloud Computing for Digital Transformation

Nowadays, the most widely used technology in transforming business environments is Cloud Computing. Cloud became mainstream in many business organisations. Adoption of Cloud by many business organisations became very rapid. Our business architecture can recommend Cloud Computing as a foundational digital transformation tool to augment the business capability of the organisation.

The most significant attribute of Cloud is that the Cloud service model can expand or reduce computer resources based on business service requirements. For example, Cloud can provide the maximum resources when the business needs a large amount of computing power, storage capacity, or network bandwidth for a specific workload at a particular timeframe. Then the business organisation can release these resources after completing a specific business mission for these workloads. This elasticity and scalability of Cloud can provide business value position for digital transformation initiatives.

'Pay per use' and 'pay as you go' are essential characteristics that Cloud services model offer. The resources can be consumed based on the business usage amount. Business use could be a short, medium, or long-term basis. For example, business consumers can pay based on computing power or storage amount they use.

Related to 'pay per use', using 'on-demand' is another characteristic of the Cloud services model. Consumers can use when they demand the required services without upfront payment or dedicated investment for the IT resources in their organisation.

The recent commercial trend for using virtual machines in publicly available Cloud services are based on three types of instances such as on-demand instance, reserved instance, and spot instance.

In on-demand instance, there is no long-term commitment. Reserved instance is a relatively longer-term with a substantial discount compared to on-demand usage. For the spot instance, as commonly promoted by several service providers, the price is agreed based on bidding.

Cloud offers resiliency to the infrastructure, applications and services. System failures such as servers or storage units can be automatically isolated with predefined instructions, and business workloads are migrated to redundant virtual units without disrupting the service levels or consumer usage. Cloud's resilience attribute removes many of business supportability concerns in digital transformation requirements.

Based on business consumer requirements, Cloud resources can be provided as virtual or physical. This flexibility is created by multitenancy characteristic of the Cloud service model. For example, a Cloud service provider can host multiple business workloads belong to different business organisations in the same infrastructure without adversely affecting their privacy and security requirements.

If there are high-security requirements such as sensitive governmental services, isolation can be on a physical basis. We need to consider architectural and business constraints and limitations which can affect the use of virtual services in multi-tenancy mode.

Flexible business workload movement is another crucial attribute of Cloud service model. There may be times a business organisation requires to run their business workloads in a different time zone, and the workloads can easily be moved to a data centre in another country.

Such business requirements may be for several reasons such as reducing cost, providing a better business service for a focus group in a different location or even business compliance and regulatory requirements. Let's introduce the next important technology, IoT, which is proliferating in many business organisations.

IoT (Internet of Things)

After Cloud Computing, another rapidly emerging technology is the IoT (Internet of Things) in many business organisations. As business architects focussing on digital transformation initiatives, we must understand the business value, use cases, and technical functions this vital technology.

Substantial progress has been made in many disciplines owing to the use of IoT in creating new business services and products. Some of these disciplines include environmental monitoring, manufacturing, infrastructure management, energy management, agriculture, healthcare, transportation, electronics, material sciences, and banking.

In many business organisations, it is noticeable that IoT technologies are emerging and IoT solutions are growing exponentially to support digital transformation initiatives.

It is estimated that billions of devices in the next few years to connect to the global IoT ecosystem. The bottom line is that IoT is valuable for both organisational business and the global economy. This is inevitable. From our current experience, we can construe that IoT can have a substantial business impact on our economy and the way we conduct business and commerce as far as digital transformation goals are concerned.

Business consumers and service providers have an incredible interest and focus on this empowering technology enabled by the internet and integrated tools and technology stacks. The generation of new business opportunities for companies and new job roles, that we cannot even name yet, is imminent.

Some believe that the IoT can be as important as the emergence of the internet itself. Some even point out that it can be the next big thing in our lives. These are, to some extent, speculations, combined with some media hype; however, time can tell as to whether the high expectations of IoT to be met. My humble opinion is yes, it can meet and even exceed the expectations.

As business architects and architecting team working for digital transformation initiatives, we need to understand IoT offerings and possess a broad range of IoT knowledge and skills because IoT is one of the primary enablers of the business digital transformation goals to create new revenue streams and broader business opportunities. After IoT, our next critical technology domain is Big Data and AI-based Analytics.

Big Data and AI-Based Analytics for Digital Transformation

In addition to IoT, Big Data and AI-based (a.k.a. Cognitive) Analytics are vital technologies and relevant business processes that we need to understand. Not only understand the business value but also, we must consider them as a business capability in our architecture framework for creating business insights and competitive advantage for our digital transformation goals.

It is important to note that even though architecturally similar to traditional data, Big Data requires newer methods and tools to deal with business data. The traditional methods and tools are not adequate to process Big Data, especially for digital transformation goals.

The Big Data process refers to capturing a substantial amount of business data from multiple sources, storing analysing, searching, transferring, sharing, updating, visualising, and governing very large volumes of data sets such as in petabytes or even exabytes nowadays.

Interestingly, the main concern or aim of Big Data is not the amount of business data but more advanced AI-based or cognitive analytics techniques to produce business value out of these large volumes of business data. The advanced analytics in this context refers to approaches such as descriptive, predictive, prescriptive, and diagnostic analytics. These types of cognitive analytics types can pose invaluable business value for our digital transformation initiatives.

We need to understand the type of analytics and when to use them for what type of business transformation solutions for our organisation. Each has a different purpose and business use cases for digital transformation goals. Let's explain briefly.

The descriptive analytics deals with situations such as what is happening right now based on incoming business data. The predictive analytics refers to what might happen in the future. Prescriptive analytics deals with actions to be taken to create business insights and value. Diagnostic analytics ask the question of why something happened within the value chain. Each analytics type serves difference scenarios and business use-cases.

AI-based Big Data Analytics is a comprehensive business-driven discipline. At a high level, it aims to make quick business decisions, reduce the cost for a business product or service, and test new market to create new business products and services.

All industries nowadays use AI-based Big Data analytics to create business value. For example, health care, life sciences, manufacturing, government, and retail are extensively using Big Data and Cognitive Analytics for new insights, creating new business opportunities, and opening new markets.

We need new methods and tools to perform AI-based Big Data analytics. There are emerging methods and many tools available on the market. Most of the methods are proprietary, but some are available via open-source programs. For our awareness and consideration in our digital transformation initiatives, some popular tools frequently mentioned in the Big Data Analytics industry publications are Aqua Data Studio, Azure HDinsight, IBM SPSS Modeler, Skytree, Talend, Splice Machine, Plotly, Lumify, Elasticsearch.

Besides, open-source has progressed well in this area and produced multiple powerful tools. Some commonly used open-source analytics tools are from Apache organisation such as Hadoop, Spark, Storm, Cassandra, and SAMOA. The other frequently used open-source tools are Neo4j, MongoDB, and R programming environment. These tools are beyond our scope in this book; however, it is useful to create awareness here as they generate business value hence widely used in digital transformation initiatives.

Big Data analytics is a broad and growing area. We can better understand Big data analytics looking at its inherent characteristics. We can summarise these characteristics using terms such as connection, conversion, cognition, configuration, content, customisation, cloud, cyber, and community. These terms are associated with our day to day business and architectural practices and self-explanatory hence we don't go into details here.

However, it can be useful to familiarise ourselves with Big Data analytics methods and techniques that we can use in our digital transformation initiatives. Some of these methods and techniques are natural language processing, data mining, association pattern mining, behavioural analytics, predictive analytics, descriptive analytics, prescriptive analytics, diagnostic analytics, and machine learning.

Machine learning is a trending discipline for AI-based Big Data Analytics. Many large business organisations have already leveraged the power of machine learning. The prime examples extensively using Machine Learning for many business-related ventures are Google and Amazon.

Machine learning refers to computer systems to learn and improve based on their learning from the analysis of large volumes of data sets without programming. It is part of the artificial intelligence domain in computer science. Due to its widespread use cases and business impact, machine learning became a vital technology and business tool for business modernisation strategies leading to digital transformation. As business architects, we need to add machine learning to our digital transformation toolbox.

Related to machine learning, we also need to understand unstructured business data handling, particularly text analytics. Text analytics take the leverage of machine learning, computational linguistics, and traditional statistical analysis. Text analytics focus on converting massive volumes of a machine or human-generated text into meaningful structures to create business insights and support business decision-making.

There are various text analytics techniques that we need to familiarise. For example, information extraction is one of the text analytics techniques which extract structured data from unstructured text. This technique can be useful for some digital transformation initiatives.

Text summarisation is another widely used unstructured data processing technique which can automatically create a condensed summary of a document or selected groups of documents. We can use text summarisation technique, especially for blogs, news, product documents, and scientific papers. There may be numerous use cases to apply text summarisation technique for digital transformation initiatives.

Natural Language Processing (NLP) is another sophisticated text analytics technique interfaced as question and answers in natural language. NLP is commonly used in various commercial products such as Siri by Apple, Watson by IBM, and Alexa by Amazon products. NLP can be an excellent enabler of some of our digital transformation goals and meet the requirements for providing natural language to our consumers.

Overall Security and Cybersecurity

In addition to analytics, security is the next critical knowledge and skill that we must possess as business architects within the digital transformation programs. Particular security, which we call cybersecurity, is even more critical in digital transformation initiatives.

Cybersecurity touches every aspect of digital transformation initiative. Cybersecurity is a vast security domain covering identity and access management, authentication, authorisation, encryption, and many more crucial areas of security management related to cyberspace. Applying cybersecurity measures is a critical success factor for securing digitally transforming business organisations.

The emerging technology stacks, especially Cloud Computing, IoT, and Big Data also mandate cybersecurity at all levels. Broader security awareness and associated skills are essential for our digital transformation initiatives.

Related to advanced security, Blockchain, which is relatively new technology, is becoming critical for new security use cases and requirements which could constitute key success factors for digital transformation goals.

Blockchain

At a high level, the Blockchain is based on a decentralised technology framework. It is digital data management protocol with a network consists of nodes. It offers storage technology coupled with information transmission.

Blockchain allows all communication participants and can be transparent to everyone involved in communications. The database of the Blockchain is distributed in nature. Its database keeps different copies simultaneously in different nodes.

The Blockchain protocol is based on peer-to-peer networking. In other words, it does not require a control body. More importantly it is believed to be infallible and extremely secure. Unlike more conventional databases, it is "distributed". It means that different copies exist simultaneously on different computers of the network by preventing the Blockchain from being hacked. It is secure by architecture, design, implementation, and operability perspectives. The security framework for the Blockchain is supported by the use of Byzantine fault tolerance.

The critical component of the Blockchain is the secure database. It has two kinds of records, namely blocks and transactions. Blocks hold batches of valid transactions. They are hashed and encoded into a Merkle tree. This is a term in cryptography. It is defined as a tree in which every non-leaf node is labelled with the cryptic hash of the labels or values of its child node.

The primary business use case for Blockchain is identity management. Blockchain can allow us to perform identity management in a decentralised manner. This powerful shift can allow us to own our data and to manage it as needed and others can trust us in the process. Blockchain is expected to evolve rapidly and transform into an inevitable and ubiquitous technology soon.

The Blockchain is still work in progress, especially in the open-source communities. These communities continually update it. There is remarkably growing interested and literature on the Blockchain in industry and by academia. Several universities have already commenced conducting substantial research in developing and extending the Blockchain to various use cases. Many large business organisations are creating awareness and make it part of their strategic business capability path. It is time for us, as business architects, to consider the business use cases and apply the Blockchain capabilities to our digital transformation goals, especially to meet new security, privacy, and business compliance requirements.

Network for Digital Transformation

As business transformation architects, we need to consider the business value and capabilities of the network within digital transformation programs. We know that digital transformation initiatives touch every aspect of networking such as wide area, local area, wireless and other networking types.

The network is a fundamental infrastructure component for any digital transformation initiatives. Networks are enablers of other critical technology stacks such as Cloud, IoT, Blockchain, and Big Data analytics. The network is so fundamental that these technology stacks cannot perform and even cannot exist without a network.

The network and associated communication technologies are the fundamental enablers of digital transformation goals. Understanding business use cases, value propositions, and the functions of network and network implications such as security, latency, bandwidth, are also important topics for the success of digital transformation initiatives. These factors play essential roles in our digital transformation initiatives.

As business architects, we need to cover broadly and sometimes in-depth based on our involvement in various digital transformation initiatives. As we usually cover the breadth, it is beneficial to leverage skills of a network architect, technical specialists, network domain experts such as CCIEs (Cisco Certified Internetwork Experts), or other network subject matter experts to help us generate business value from the network.

Mobility

Mobility is a critical interrelated technology domain in digitally transforming organisations, moving to mobile solutions. As business architects, we need to understand and educate our architecting teams for the effective use of mobility for innovations leading to business insights and collaboration across the business organisation including our customers and partners.

We also need to understand the domain of Enterprise Mobile Management for digital transformation. This domain includes essential components such as device management, application management, content management, email management, and unified endpoint management.

Mobility is associated with several architectural and business considerations such as network access, compliance, data management, workplace demographics, end-user accountability and BYOD (Bring Your Own Devices) practices in many organisations.

IT Service Management

IT service management is inevitable for transforming business organisations. IT service management covers an extensive array of technology, business process, and technical tools. IT service management includes processes such as change management, problem management, incident management, service level management, capacity management, availability management, business continuity management, and security management.

In addition, system management processes such as monitoring, alerting and event management can be covered under the umbrella term of IT Service Management. These processes are managed using many technological tools. More importantly, these tools need to be architected, integrated, designed and implemented coherently aligned with business architecture framework and supporting digital transformation goals.

Understanding the dynamics of these tools within the context of digital transformation initiatives are vital for successful business outcomes.

One of the best representations of IT Service model is implemented using popular ITIL (Information Technology Infrastructure Library. Knowledge of ITIL can be handy in communicating our service management needs to broader stakeholders in the digitally transforming business organisation.

Chapter 9: Data for Digital Transformation

Purpose

As business architects, we know that data is the most valuable asset for business intelligence. For valid reasons, there is tremendous focus on data quality, availability, and integration for successful digital transformation initiatives.

Leveraging data intelligence steers the digital transformation in the right direction and leads to new business insights. One significant fact is that data, especially Big Data, is ubiquitous in every enterprise.

Large organisations generate massive amounts of data coming from multiple sources. There are ongoing real-time data collection and analysis creating business value. The most prominent example is the data coming from embedded objects as we discussed in the IoT technology section.

As business architects and architecting team, data is our bread and butter for our digital transformation initiatives. Therefore, we need to understand every aspect of data in its lifecycle methodically. Let's start with Big Data.

Big Data for Digital Transformation

Big data is different from traditional data. The main differences come from characteristics such as volume, velocity, variety, veracity, value and overall complexity of data sets in a data platform or overall business ecosystem. Let's touch on these five V terms to understand the nature of Big Data. These V terms can be very useful mnemonics to remember the characteristics of the Big Data.

Let's start with volume. Volume refers to the size or amount of data sets. We can measure them in terabytes, petabytes or exabytes. There are no specific definitions to determine the threshold for Big Data volumes. Ironically, even though it is called the Big Data, and it is a signifier, the volume is not the main characteristics of the Big Data as far as architecture, design, and deployments are concerned.

Velocity refers to the speed of producing data. Big Data sources generate high-speed data streams coming from real-time devices such as mobile phones, social media, IoT sensors, IoT edge gateways, and the Cloud data stores. Velocity is an essential factor in all phases of the Big Data architecture and management considerations.

Variety refers to multiple sources of data. The data sources include structured transactional data, semi-structured data such as web sites or system logs, and unstructured data such as video, audio, animation, and pictures. Variety is also a significant factor for Big Data architecture and data management considerations.

Veracity means the quality of the data. Since volume and velocity are enormous in Big Data, maintaining veracity can be very challenging. It is essential to have quality output to make sense of data for business insights. Veracity is also related to value.

Value is the primary purpose of Big Data to create new insights and gain business value from Big Data. We can create business value with innovative and creative approaches performed by all the stakeholders of Big Data solutions.

Overall complexity for Big Data refers to more data attributes and difficulty to extract desired value due to large volume, wide variety, enormous velocity, and required veracity for the desired business value.

Even though architecturally similar to traditional data from a lifecycle management perspective, Big Data requires newer methods and tools to deal with data. The traditional methods and tools are not adequate to process Big Data.

The Big Data process refers to capturing a substantial amount of data from multiple sources, storing, analysing, searching, transferring, sharing, updating, visualising, and governing huge volumes of data sets in the magnitude of petabytes or even exabytes.

The main concern or aim of Big Data is not the amount of data but more advanced analytics techniques to produce business value out of these large volumes of data sets. The advanced analytics in this context refers to approaches such as descriptive, predictive, prescriptive, and diagnostic analytics. Let's re-iterate the meaning of these analytics techniques in a summary as they are crucial for digital transformation initiatives.

The descriptive analytics deals with situations such as what is happening right now based on incoming data. The predictive analytics refers to what might happen in the future. Prescriptive analytics deals with actions to be taken. Diagnostic analytics ask the question of why something happened. Each analytics type serves different scenarios and use-cases. Now, let's touch on the data management lifecycle.

Data Management Lifecycle

Understanding full data lifecycle management can be useful for business architects. Data is a critical aspect of business organisations. As business architects we need to understand business value and function of data for our organisations. Especially for digital transformation initiatives, we can consider Big Data as a critical player in program level, the enterprise level, and the organisation's information ecosystem level.

Our roles and responsibilities may differ in different stages in the lifecycle; however, we need to be on top of the life cycle management, especially from the governance perspective, throughout the digital transformation initiatives.

A typical Big Data architecture, similar to traditional data lifecycle, includes several distinct phases in the overall data lifecycle management. As business architects in the digital transformation program, we can participate in all phases of the lifecycle, providing different input for each stage.

Data is a key business domain that business architects need to understand deeply. Enterprise architects or transformation architects, depending on the structure of the transformation program can create a standard naming convention for the phases to bring everyone on the same page.

Let's keep in mind that there is no rigorous universal systematic approach to the Big Data lifecycle as the discipline is still evolving. Names and approaches are continually changing based on ongoing experimentations.

At a high level, the data management lifecycle can include foundations, acquisitions, preparation, input, processing, output, interpretation, analytics, consumptions, retention, backup, recovery, archival, and destruction.

As business architects, we may get involved in some of these stages; hence, a broad knowledge of these phases can be beneficial to gain data management awareness. Let's briefly touch on the phases.

Foundation phase includes understanding and validating data requirements, solution scope, roles and responsibilities of stakeholders, data infrastructure preparation, technical and non-technical considerations, and understanding data rules in an organisation.

The foundation phase requires a detailed plan facilitated ideally by a project manager with substantial input from the Big Data solution architects and guidance from business architects in the digital transformation program. A PDR (project definition report) must cover the non-technical matters such as project funding, commercials, and other issues. Enterprise architects govern this phase at the enterprise level, and transformation architects cover it within the transformation program scope. Business architects provide a framework for business use of the Big Data.

Data Acquisition phase refers to collecting data. We can obtain data from various sources. These sources can be internal and external to the organisation. Data sources can be structured forms such as transferred from a data warehouse, transaction systems, or semi-structured forms such as Web or system logs, or unstructured such as media files consist of videos, audios, and pictures.

Data governance, security, privacy, and quality controls start with the data collection phase. The lead data architects document the data collection strategy, requirements, architectural decisions, use cases, and technical specifications in this phase. Transformation architects may need to review and approve the requirements and architectural decisions affecting the digital transformation initiatives. Data and platform specialists review and approve the specifications.

In the data preparation phase, we clean the collected raw data. We check the data rigorously for any inconsistencies, errors, and duplicates. We consistently remove any redundant, duplicated, incomplete, and incorrect data sets and entries. This activity results in having a clean data set for business use. Preparation of data is usually a specialist level task; however, business architects may need to govern this phase with input from the business stakeholders. We can delegate specific activities to the data solution architects and specialists.

Data input refers to sending data to planned target data repositories or systems. For example, we send the clean data to determined destinations such as CRM systems, data lakes, or data warehouse. In this phase, we transform the raw data into a useable format. Usually, an Enterprise architect governs this phase; business and transformation architects may get involved in architecture board review activities.

Data Processing starts with processing the raw form of data. Then, we convert data into a readable format giving it the form and context. After this activity, we can interpret data by the selected data analytics tools. We can use generic or proprietary Big Data processing tools based on the data practices in our business organisation.

Some standard tools that we may deal with are Hadoop MapReduce, Impala, Hive, Pig, and Spark SQL. The most commonly used real-time data processing tool is HBase, and near real-time data processing tools is Spark Streaming. Data processing also includes activities such as data annotation, integration, aggregation, and representation.

In this phase, data may change its format based on requirements. We can use processed data in various data outputs such as in data lakes, for enterprise networks, and connected devices. We can further analyse data using advanced processing techniques and tools such as Spark MLib, Spark GraphX, and machine learning.

Data processing activities may require various team members with different skills sets. While the lead Big Data solution architect leads the phase, data specialists, engineers, and data scientists perform most of the activities. Enterprise architects govern this phase from approach, process, technology and tool perspective with input from the business architects dealing with business stakeholders. Business and transformation architects participate in governance activities for digital transformation programs.

Data output is a phase where the data is in a format ready for consumption by the business users. We can transform data into useable formats such as plain text, graphs, processed images or video files. This phase announces the data ready for use and sends the data to the next stage for storing.

Data output phase in some organisation is also called data ingestion aiming to export data for immediate use or future use and keep it in a database format. Ingestion process can be a real-time or batch format. We must familiarise ourselves with standard Big Data ingestion tools such as Sqoop, Flume, and Spark streaming.

Once we complete the data output phase, we store data in allocated storage units as pointed out by the data platform designs. Once data is stored, then it can be easily accessed by the defined business user groups. Big Data storage includes underlying technologies such as relational data storage or extended data storage such as HDFS and HBASE.

We can consider the file formats text, binary, or another type of specialised formats such as Sequence, Avro, and Parquet in data storage phase. Several architects and specialists participate in this phase. While business and transformation architects work with the enterprise architects to set the standards, infrastructure architects build the data platforms with the input from the data or information architects.

Once the data is stored, in traditional models, it ends the process. However, for Big Data, there may be a need for the integration of stored data for various purposes. Some data analytics models may require the use of data ponds and lakes integrated with data warehouses or data marts.

There may also be application integration requirements. For example, some integration activities may comprise of integrating data with dashboards, tableau, websites, or data visualisations applications.

This activity may overlap with the next phase, which is data analytics.

Transformed and integrated data is ready for data analytics, which is the next phase. Data analytics is a significant component of Big Data. This phase is critical because we gain business insights and value from Big Data. There can be a team responsible for data analytics led by a data scientist. Data architect has a limited role in this phase. Data architects need to ensure we complete this phase using architectural rigour for analytics. Enterprise architects validate the standards with input from business architects. Transformation architects can provide guidance and requirements clarification of analytics within their scope.

Once data analytics takes place, then we turn data into information ready for consumption by the internal or external users, including customers of the business organisation. Some critical data may need to be backed up. There are data backup strategies, techniques, methods and tools that, as business architects, we may need to provide with guidance to identify, document, and obtain approval in the digital transformation programs.

We may need to archive some critical data for regulatory or other business reasons for a defined period. With the input from business architects working with the business stakeholders, the enterprise or transformation architects determine, and document data retention strategy approved by the governing body in the data practice department.

There may be regulatory requirements to destruct a particular type of data after a certain amount of times. These may change based on the industries that data belong. Even though there is a chronological order for the life cycle management, for producing Big Data solutions, some phases may slightly overlap; hence, we can perform them in parallel.

The life cycle provided in this chapter is a guideline and can be customised based on the structure of the data practice team, data business requirements, and dynamics of the owner business organisation's departments or at their overall enterprise level.

Usually, data architects begin with an understanding of the process end to end. We can classify the process under two broad categories. The first one is Data Management, and the second one is Data Analytics.

As business architects, it can be useful for us to understand data management activities such as data acquisition, extraction, cleansing, annotation, processing, integration, aggregation, and representation activities. We also need to understand data analytics activities such as modelling, analysis, interpretation, and visualisation at a high level.

Data Platforms for Digital Transformation

As business architects, it can be useful to understand the function of data platforms in our digital transformation initiatives. The first layer of the data platform is the shared operational information zone consists of the data types such as data in motion, data at rest, and data in several other forms.

This first layer includes legacy data sources, new data sources, master data hubs, reference data hubs, and content repositories.

The second large layer is processing. This layer includes data ingestion, operational information, landing area, analytics zone, archive, real-time analytics, exploration, integrated warehouse, data mart zones.

The second layer needs to have a governance model for metadata catalogue including data security and disaster recovery of systems, storage and hosting and other infrastructure components such as Cloud.

The third layer is the analytics platform. It consists of real-time analytics, planning, forecasting, decision making, predictive analytics, data discovery, visualisations, dashboard, and other analytics features.

The fourth layer consists of outputs such as business processes, decision-making schemes, and point of interactions. We need to provide access with established controls both for the data platform professionals such as data scientists, data architects, analytics experts, and business users. We need to engage a security architect or subject matter experts to analyse the requirements and take appropriate measures.

Level of the schema for the data platform is a crucial architectural consideration. We can classify the level of schema under three categories, such as no schema, partially structured schema, and full structured schema. Control of schema is an enterprise concern; therefore, enterprise architects need to take control of this function with input from business and transformation architects.

To understand the type of schema, we can use examples. Some examples of no schema are video, audio and picture files; social media feed, partial schema such as email, instant messaging logs, system logs, call centre logs; and high schema can be structured sensor data and relational transaction data.

The data processing levels require business architectural considerations. The processing levels could be raw data, validated data, transformed data and calculated data. Another structural classification of data in this platform is related the business relevance. We can categorise the business relevance of data as external data, personal data, departmental data and enterprise data.

Business Vocabulary

Another essential concept in data management is business vocabulary. We need to define business vocabulary as a shared understanding of Big Data related to business analytics.

Business vocabulary provides consistent terms to be used by the whole organisation. Business departments own business vocabulary. Enterprise Architects ensure that this is in place and adequately governed with input from business architects.

Usually, business users maintain this vocabulary. This vocabulary describes the business content supported by the data models. More importantly, from an architectural perspective, this vocabulary can be a crucial input to the metadata catalogue; hence, it can be a business enterprise concern or digital transformation program concern.

Data Governance in Digital Transformation

As business architects, we work with enterprise architects to govern data in our digital transformation programs. Data governance is a critical factor for digital transformation programs.

For the Big Data governance, we need to consider essential factors such as security, privacy, trust, operability, conformance, agility, innovation and transformation of data.

It is also vital that at a fundamental level, a data governance infrastructure to be established and evolve for adoption at the digital transformation program or enterprise level in an integrated manner.

Data governance may take consideration for different stakeholders in the enterprise and its data ecosystem. For example, data architects are responsible for developing the governance of Big Data models with business input from business architects. Data scientists are accountable for an analytics perspective. Business stakeholders are responsible for the governance of business models for producing business results for the data ecosystem in concern. As business architects, we establish the bridge between the business and governing architecture team.

Big Data governance is a broad area and covers components, scope, requirements handling, strategy, business architecture, technical design, application development, data analysis, quality tests, processing, components, relationships, input, output, business goals, business insights, and all other aspects of data management and analytics.

As business architects, we must closely work with enterprise architects and other architecture team members to maintain governance in digital transformation programs. Enterprise Architects are responsible for end to end governance of Big Data architecture and the associated solutions at the enterprise level. They may delegate some governance tasks with Big Data lead, business architects, and solution architects as required. As business architects, our focus is always on the digitally transforming business environments within our scope.

Data Lakes for Digital Transformation

Big Data digital transformation solutions require the use of the data lake model. Data lakes are fundamental and useful aspects of Big Data lifecycle management. Let's define and explain this important component which can be a critical part of our digital ecosystem.

We can define data lakes in the simplest terms as the raw and instantly useable data sources made available for specific purposes.

The need for data lakes come from users to take advantage of clean data based on self-service approach without needing technical data professionals. Use of data lakes can be a critical business proposition for digital transformation programs.

A data lake can be a single store of transformed enterprise data in the native format. They are usually well reported, visualised and analysed using advanced analytics. A data lake can include structured, semi-structured, and unstructured data such as images, videos, or sounds.

Data lakes are dynamic stores and can be fed iteratively as further clean data are discovered and transformed from multiple sources in the enterprise.

For example, a data lake can store relational data from enterprise applications and non-relational data from IoT devices, social media, and mobile apps.

There are multiple use cases for data lakes. The most common ones are when real-time data analysis required for the data sources coming from various sources. Another use case can be related to the goals of having a complete view of customer data coming from multiple sources. Auditing requirements and centralisation of data can also be use cases for data lakes. These use cases are relevant and can be significant for digital transformation goals.

The business value of data lakes come from being able to perform advanced analytics very quickly for data coming from various real-time sources such as clickstreams, social media, system logs. Use of data lakes helps the business stakeholders to identify opportunities rapidly, make informed decisions, and act on their decision expeditiously for speed to the market.

Data lakes can be implemented using various tools, techniques, and services. There are commercially available services as well as open-source services to establish data lakes. For example, commercial products such as Azure Data Lake, Amazon S3 and open source product Apache Hadoop file system are some data lake implementation enablers to consider for our solutions. There are many more tools and methods to design, implement and execute data lake solutions.

Based on feedback obtained from many successful implementations of data lakes, it appears that an excellent choice of platform for data lakes is Hadoop. Hadoop, as an open-source system, is highly scalable, modular, technology agnostic, cost-effective and presents no schema limitations. I observed that many architects I worked with and met in other organisations embraced Hadoop due to its effectiveness for transformations.

Designing data lakes require critical consideration of data types. For example, one key consideration is that if the purpose of data is unknown, it is better to keep data in raw format so that it can be used by data professionals in the future when it is needed. As business architects we need to understand the use cases of data lakes and the transformation architects can guide architectural decisions at the program level as far as digital transformations are concerned.

One of the critical challenges of data lakes is security as the data comes to the lake in real-time from multiple uncontrolled sources. To address this challenge, a well-governing security architecture with access controls and semantic consistency need to be in place for the enterprise data lake.

Data lake design is a specialist level activity usually conducted by an experienced storage architect or specialist. Transformation architects may provide input to set the standards and maintain the governance for the lifecycle of data lake initiatives.

In addition to data lakes, we also need to understand the data puddles and ponds. Data puddle is a tiny purpose-build data platform usually used by a specific single team mission in an organisation conducted by a marketing group or data scientist. They are also a right candidate for data-intensive ETL (Extract, Transform, Load) offloading engagements for a single team. Unlike data lakes, they are not data-driven processing allowing informed decisions at enterprise levels.

Related to data puddles, another term used for a group of data puddles is data ponds. We can design data ponds for a small amount of data management purposes. One way of explaining a data pond is to resemble it to a data warehouse designed for Big Data processing.

One more essential term related to data lakes that we need to understand is 'data swamp'. This term refers to an unmanaged data lake that may not be accessible by the intended consumers or may not provide desired business value. From lessons learned in the field, many unsuccessful implementations of data lakes, unfortunately, turned into data swamps.

Let's keep in mind that data swamps are undesirable situations in an enterprise and digital transformation initiatives. Thus, as transformation architects, we need to consider these types of hard-learned lessons for data management strategy of the digital transformation plans.

Business Data Considerations for Digital Transformation

As business architects, we leverage business and architectural skills, relevant technology, and tools to create custom solutions, such as 'data products', for digital transformations. The custom solutions can be data products or services depending on the goals and the scope of the digital transformation programs.

Big Data solutions in digital transformation programs are distinct and require additional expertise. In addition to considering several architectural points, these data solutions also require domain knowledge of data and information architecture.

At the highest level, we need to identify optimal approaches to collecting, storing, processing, analysing, and presenting Big Data. However, practical solutions are architected by Big Data or Information Architects with our guiding input.

Big Data solutions require heterogeneous technology and tools to fit the purpose. It is essential to realise that there is no single technology or tool which can provide all-purpose for developing Big Data solutions in digital transformation programs.

Besides, due to their dependencies and relationships to many components, attributes, and factors, Big Data solutions cannot be developed in isolation or silos. With input from business architects, the transformation architects need to consider the entire ecosystem and break the data silos in thinking and critical architectural factors that may affect the whole digital transformation program.

For Big Data solutions, we must focus on highly scalable platforms, processes, technology, and tools. Due to its nature, scalability is a fundamental requirement for Big Data solutions. Compromising scalability, even in a small amount, can cause undesirable solutions, troubled projects, and failed service levels. Scalability is a critical factor for digital transformation initiatives.

Modularity is another essential consideration for Big Data solutions for digital transformation goals. For modularity, we need to ensure the modules fits into the big picture. For example, the same data should be able to be used by different projects in a program and technology stacks rather than creating unnecessary data access silos.

Big Data solutions for digital transformation requires thinking out of the box and innovative ways of doing things. We need to understand the latest technologies and practices for Big Data solutions. For example, there is a trend in the industry for trying new methods of data analysis without binding to traditional EDW (electronic data warehouse) resources and ETL (extract transform load) processes.

In terms of tools and technologies, we can consider mixing open source and commercial systems based on their applicability and meeting our requirements. For example, OLTP (online transaction processing) can be designed using commercially available relational databases for structured and open-source Casandra database supporting semi-structured databases.

Data sources in business organisations keep changing, and new sources are being available. In addition to legacy data sources, we need to consider new data sources in Big Data modernisation and digital transformation initiatives. We need to determine the type of data sources required in our digital transformation programs.

From solution readiness and quality management perspectives, it is vital to determine the timelines of data ingestion in the enterprise. Data ingestion, as a critical aspect of Big Data in the modernisation and transformation context, is the process of importing, transferring, loading processing and storing data for use.

Data can be transferred as synchronous, or an asynchronous batched, or real-time basis. We need to articulate these options with compelling reasons and obtain validating input and approvals from subject matter experts and the solution governance body.

It is vital to choose the type of processing to perform whether real-time or batch processing. Our data processing may involve descriptive, predictive, prescriptive, diagnostic, and ad-hoc. We also need to consider the latency expectation of processing. These factors can plan an important role in digital transformation initiatives.

We need to determine how to access the data, for example, by random or sequential order. Besides, we need to consider data access patterns. Data access patterns are necessary to optimise data access requirements. There are many patterns available in data application integration and interface publications. For example, some common patterns are accelerating database resource initialisation, eliminating data access bottlenecks, and hiding obscure database semantics from data users.

Database optimisation is an essential practice at the enterprise level. These techniques aim to improve the quality and speed for data access, read and write activities. Some of the critical considerations are using appropriate indexes, removing unnecessary indexes and minimising data transfers from client to server.

So far, we touched on a very high-level view of business data considerations at the program and the enterprise level. These are the only tip of the iceberg in developing Big Data solutions for digital transformation initiatives.

With input from business architects, transformation architects provide high-level guidance without going into the details of Big Data design and deployment as it is specialist-level solution expertise rather than business, program, or enterprise-level concern.

Once we start the process and delve into requirements, we can come across many more considerations based on our industry, program goals, and many other technical factors which some of them can be beyond our controls and may require domain expertise.

Therefore, it is essential to follow an established data management method, a collaborative solution team, proven processes, leading technology stacks, and well-supported tools to produce successful Big Data solutions for digital transformations.

As business architects, we can guide the team with our knowledge of these critical foundational data practices and business value understanding, and we always stay on top of the program level business data requirements for our digital transformation initiatives.

As we recommend the use of a lot of open-source data platform products and tools, it can be beneficial to further understand the importance of open-source for our digital transformation programs.

Open Source Data Platforms

I want to highlight the importance of using open-source tools for digital transformation initiatives, especially in the data platforms. Use of open source tools can be very beneficial for digital transformation programs.

We all are aware of open source but due to its importance, let's briefly touch on the commonly used and recommended Big Data tools in the open-source space.

Open source is incredibly useful and widespread for information technology hence equally crucial for data analytics in the enterprise. It is a type of licensing agreement which allows the developers and users to freely use the software, modify it, develop new ways to improve it and integrate to larger projects. It is a collaborative and innovative approach embraced by many business organisations. It is not only ideal for start-up companies and those companies with a tight IT budget but also business organisations struggling to have more flexible architectures for digital transformation initiatives.

There are many open-source tools and technologies for Big Data and Analytics. Being familiar with some essential and commonly used open-source tools can be useful. An awareness of these tools is fundamental for us.

Here's a summary of the famous open-source Big Data and Analytics tools. Let's start with famous Hadoop. Apache Hadoop is a platform for data storage and processing. Hadoop is scalable, fault-tolerant, flexible, cost-effective and open source. It is ideal for handling massive storage pools using the batch approach in distributed computing environments. We can use Hadoop for complex Big Data and Analytics solutions at the enterprise level.

The next is Cassandra. Apache Cassandra is a semi-structured open source database. It is linearly scalable, high speed, and fault-tolerant. The primary use case for Cassandra is a transactional system requiring fast response and massive scalability. Cassandra is also widely used for Big Data and Analytics solutions at the enterprise level.

Apache Kafka is a stream processing software platform. Using Kafka, users can subscribe to commit logs and publish data to any number of systems or real-time applications. Kafka offers a unified, high-throughput, low-latency platform for real-time handling data feeds. Kafka platforms were initially developed by LinkedIn, used for a while, and donated to open source.

Apache Flume offers a simple and flexible architecture. The architecture of Flume is a reliable, distributed software for efficiently collecting, aggregating, and moving large amounts of log data in the Big Data ecosystem. We can use Flume for streaming data flows. Flume is fault-tolerant with many failover and recovery systems. Flume uses an extensible data model that allows for online analytic application.

Apache NiFi is an automation tool designed to automate the flow of data amongst the software components based on flow-based programming model. Currently, Cloudera supports for its commercial and development requirements. It has a portal for the users and uses TLS encryption for security.

Apache Samza is a near-real-time stream processing system. It provides an asynchronous framework for stream processing. Samza allows building stateful applications that process data in real-time from multiple sources. It is well known for offering fault tolerance, stateful processing, and isolation.

Apache Sqoop is a command-line interface application used to transfer data between Apache Hadoop and the relational databases. We can use it for incremental loads of a single table or free form SQL queries. We can use Sqoop with Hive and HBase to populate the tables.

Apache Chukwa is a system for data collection. Chukwa monitors large distributed systems and builds on the MapReduce framework on HDFS (Hadoop Distributed File System). Chukwa is a scalable, flexible and robust system for data collection.

Apache Storm is a stream processing framework. The Storm is based on spouts and bolts to define data sources. It allows batch and distributed processing of streaming data. The Storm also enables real-time data processing.

Apache Spark is a framework that allows cluster computing for distributed environments. We can use Spark for general clustering needs. It provides fault tolerance and data parallelism. Spark's architectural foundation is based on the resilient distributed dataset. The Dataframe API is an abstraction on top of the resilient distributed dataset. Spark has different editions, such as Core, SQL, Streaming, and GraphX.

Apache Hive is a data warehouse software. We can build Hive on Hadoop platform. Hive provides data query and supports the analysis of large datasets stored in HDFS. It offers a query language called HiveQL.

Apache HBase is a non-relational distributed database. HBase runs on top of HDFS. HBase provides Google's Bigtable-like capabilities for Hadoop. HBase is a fault-tolerant system.

Another great tool, non-Apache is MongoDB. It is a high performance, fault-tolerant, scalable, cross-platform and NoSQL database. It deals with unstructured data. It is developed by MongoDB Inc is licensed under the SSPL (Server-Side Public License), which is a kind of open-source product.

There are many more rapidly developing open-source software tools which can be used for various functions of data life cycle management in the enterprise. These tools can be handy for transformation programs focusing on Big Data and Analytics solutions. These tools are easily accessible and available based on open source licencing agreements.

Commercial Big Data and Analytics Tools

There are also many commercially available tools and technologies for Big Data and Analytics suitable to deploy across enterprise-wide solutions. These tools and technologies can be sold as products or services.

As transformation architects, we need to be aware of these products and services as they can be beneficial for our digital transformation initiatives.

Some of the most popular Big Data and Analytics platforms with associated tools are Google BigQuery, Hortonworks Data Platform, HP Bigdata, IBM Big Data, Microsoft Azure, SAP Bigdata Analytics, Teradata Bigdata Analytics, Amazon Web Services.

As coverage of these platforms and tools is comprehensive and exhaustive, it is beyond the scope of this book to include them here. I highly recommend reading the white papers of these products before imitating your architectural activities and especially before making any architectural decisions.

Chapter 10: Mobility for Digital Transformation

Purpose

We use and work with mobile devices every day. Mobility is critical to achieving digital transformation goals. Mobile business computing is so crucial that the whole digital transformation approach revolves around the mobility of business products and services. We need to architect mobility with the utmost care and rigorous, methodical approach with substantial input from business stakeholders.

Importance of Mobility

Mobility involves people, process, technology and tools at a massive scale in every business organisation. Mobility is essential for business users and their work engagements to be productive.

The demand for mobility is rapidly increasing in business environments. The process for mobility is also challenged to meet the demands of business consumers. In one way or another, everyone in our consumer society is affected by mobile technology and processes.

Mobile technology and tools are proliferating on the market. Mobile devices, mobile phones, mobile computers, tablets, wireless networks are a few to mention. It is not feasible to have a digital transformation initiative without extensively using mobile technology stacks and tools in consumer product and services.

Mobility Lifecycle Management

Lifecycle management for mobile devices is an essential architectural consideration in digital transformation initiatives. Managing mobile devices can be daunting from many angles. The life cycle for mobile devices can be much shorter than traditional computing and telecommunication devices.

One of the primary challenges related to the lifecycle of mobile devices is dealing with quantity. In the past, there were only office phones and employees used to share them. Nowadays, employees have multiple mobile phones. Having multiple mobile devices per person may equate to thousands of mobile devices to consider at the program and enterprise level.

In addition to quantity, the users in the organisations may change their mobile devices frequently. These frequent changes may require consideration of applications and software updates for these devices in a dynamic lifecycle.

Digital transformation strategies must consider the challenges associated with the lifecycle of these mobile devices. As business architects, we need to create dynamic and flexible governance to address the concerns related to the use and lifecycle management of these devices in our digital transformation initiatives.

Mobile Security Implications

The security implications of mobile devices pose massive challenges. They create many security vulnerabilities for enterprises. Software updates can be persistent and very frequent. Frequent updates and patching can create massive workloads for the business and IT support departments. These challenges inevitably affect our digital transformation programs.

Use of these mobile devices increases information consumption in the enterprise dramatically. Security control of the data can be daunting too. These security implications cross the data and application domains; hence, a collaborative effort among the security, data and application architects are required. As business architects, we must coordinate this collaboration across business, technical, and architectural domains in our programs.

These critical challenges created by mobile devices are real and evident in the digital transformation programs. Therefore, digital transformation programs must consider these challenges and find practical and innovative ways to address them. We touched the importance of cybersecurity concerns in previous chapters.

Mobile Business Intelligence

Mobile business intelligence, also known as Mobile BI is an essential requirement for business organisations to stay competitive, open new markets, and create new revenue streams. Mobile BI includes both real-time and historical information for analysing mobile devices such as phones and tablets. The primary purpose of Mobile BI is to provide insights, based on past and current information, for business decision making.

Mobile BI is necessary for the overall support of mobile devices in the transforming ecosystem. This intelligence, providing a broad perspective on the business data, sales figures, consumption figures, and performance statistics can be valuable for digital transformation initiatives.

Using the analytics on mobile progress in digital transformation initiatives can be instrumental for developing new business models and improving the current models.

Product and service providers widely use Mobile BI. Some established and popular Mobile BI environments are publicly accessible services such as Appstore by Apple, Google Play Store, and Samsung Galaxy Store.

Our digital transformation programs can model these well-functioning services to create and improve our current Mobile BI strategy, business service models, and business offerings.

Unified Endpoint Management

A unified endpoint management (UEM) practice is an essential requirement for digital transformation initiatives. UEM includes necessary software tools and centralised management interfaces for business consumers. This centralisation is required to improve the security capabilities and also allow a collaborative content sharing for the business consumers and other stakeholders. We need to integrate unified endpoint management to our digital transformation program structure.

Other Considerations for Mobility

Mobility is an inevitable part of our digital transformation programs. It creates a bridge for employees between homes and workplaces. In some ways, employers can easily access their employees; however, the privacy of employees are affected by this easy accessibility. This privacy issue needs to be addressed in the digital transformation program.

As a matter of fact, we cannot do business without the use of mobile devices anymore. Mobility is an essential part of business organisations and digital transformation programs. Mobility touches every aspect of the workplace. We cannot have a digital business workplace without proper mobility architecture in place.

We cannot transform our legacy enterprise without including the mobility to the equation. Due to these compelling reasons, we must approach mobility from business, strategic, and architectural perspectives to properly integrate it into the business culture and digitally transforming ecosystem of our business organisations.

Chapter 11: Smart Objects for Digital Transformation

Purpose

Our purpose in this chapter is to discuss the importance of smart objects combined with the power of the Internet. Yes, as you may guess, we are talking about the Internet of Things (IoT). IoT is one of the major pillars in our digital transformation method. As IoT is ubiquitous, it is an inevitable factor for the success of our digital transformation goals.

IoT Business Value Propositions

The main benefit and business value proposition of IoT come from collecting an enormous amount of data from various means and devices in the enterprise and then building services based on analyses of these massive amounts of data. Developing new services from such a collection of data would result in a substantial outcome with multiple architectural and business implications.

Business organisations quickly accepted IoT as key-value preposition because it helps our organisation to predict the future gains; hence, the more data provided by the IoT systems, the better the analyses and outcomes can be. These data-rich analyses help us predict the future better, manage risks, and intervene before any potential damage occurs.

As we can synthesise IoT data via cognitive analytics, IoT solutions can help our business gain better insights from structured, semi-structured, unstructured, dynamic or static data by integrating with cognitive systems.

Like humans, a cognitive system undertakes the duties of learning, understanding, planning, problem-solving, deciding, analysing, synthesising and assessing.

We can use IoT solutions in many facets of digital transformation programs. IoT solutions can be used for transformation of department, enterprise-wide, and external entities to the enterprise to predict what we need and want.

For digital transformation purposes, as an extended electronic ecosystem, IoT solutions can help to eliminate cumbersome technology adversely affecting the performance of our organisations.

IoT can offer several applications at large scale for enterprises serving different industries. Some typical applications of IoT solutions are industrial control, robotics, medical, workplace safety, and security, embedded sensing in buildings, remote control, traffic control and most recently self-driving cars.

Architectural Implications of IoT Data

From an architectural perspective, we need to be aware that IoT devices generate massive amounts of data on an ongoing basis. These data sets go to the full data management life cycle; for example, in storing, analysing, re-building, and archiving.

Considering the scalability requirements for digital transformations, we must carefully consider the amount of data produced by IoT devices. The voluminous data in the enterprise require careful performance, scalability, usability, security, and availability measures.

When dealing with IoT in the digital transformation programs, as transformation architects, we must take the responsibility of data management requirements at the program level. We need to simulate the actual workload models based on the functional and non-functional requirements. We also need to consider historical data and future growth as part of the requirements analysis for performance.

Due to potential implications for enterprise and our transformation programs, we must plan data collection via IoT sensors carefully. First, we need to determine the type of physical signals to measure.

Then, we need to identify the number of sensors to be used and the speed of signals for these sensors in our data acquisition plan. Transformation architects need to closely work with the IoT Solution Architects to create stringent governance around data collection plans.

In addition to the challenges of massive data, application usage patterns are also an essential factor for the performance of IoT business solutions in the digital transformation initiatives. In particular, the processors and memory of the servers hosting the IoT applications need to be considered carefully using benchmarks.

Using benchmarks for application, data, and infrastructure, we need to create an exclusive IoT performance model and a set of test strategies for our transformation solutions.

The IoT performance model mandates more data storage capacity, faster processes, more memory, and faster network infrastructure. While in the traditional performance models, we mainly consider user simulations, in the IoT Performance models, we also consider the simulation of devices, sensors, and actuators across the enterprise.

From a data management perspective, it is paramount to be aware of data frequency shared amongst devices. We need to consider not only the amount of data produced and processed but also accessed and shared frequently by multiple entities of the IoT ecosystem.

We must be mindful that the monitoring of these devices also creates a tremendous amount of data. If we always add the alerts and other system management functions to keep these devices well-performing and available, we need to have a comprehensive performance model, including the system and service management of the complex IoT ecosystem. IoT solutions for digital transformation initiatives span across data, security, application and integration architectures.

IoT Cloud for Digital Transformation

We covered the importance of Cloud Computing and the industry trends in previous chapters. As Cloud marked a paradigm shift to Information Technology and Computing field, the IoT Cloud is a critical player in the ecosystem to enable digital transformation capabilities. The central role the Cloud plays in IoT is to facilitate the data integration of the solution components for digital transformation goals.

IoT solutions are mainly used to provide real-time information to consumers. The data required to generate real-time data can be massive in scale. The Cloud, along with computing power, storage, analytics, metering, and billing components, can make this information available for our customers effectively.

One of the business value propositions of IoT for digital transformation initiatives is the integration of Cloud to IoT, which can create new revenue streams for the organisation.

Integrating the Cloud with the IoT can create new business models enriched by real-time analysis and directly-consumed information at the same time. In other words, without the Cloud, the IoT can hardly add any value due to its real-time data and information-rich nature.

The addition of the Cloud to the IoT can also contribute to improved security, availability and performance of the IoT solutions in the modernising and transforming enterprise. Cloud providers have rigorous security, availability and performance metrics established based on a service consumption model. In particular, IoT-enabled Cloud systems seem to pose additional security measures.

Another architectural consideration is the use of Edge computing. When integrated with Edge computing, Cloud computing can add better value to the IoT ecosystem. The main reason for this is that Edge computing can do the filtering for the Cloud to focus on the usable data.

As transformation architects, we need to understand Cloud Computing architecture and how to integrate it into IoT solutions at the program level. Being aware of the transforming capabilities of Cloud technologies can be beneficial in creating large-scale commercial IoT solutions for digital transformation initiatives.

Implications of IoT Analytics Computation

IoT solutions need computers to perform analytics and intelligence activities. Such tasks are hosted by Cloud platforms, such as analytics applications in which computation performance is essential.

We also need to consider the implication of massive data for storage platform performance. For analytics storage, we need to make an architectural decision as to whether local storage or cloud-based storage can suit our requirements. This architectural decision is necessary to address cost and performance concerns at the program level.

We can consider using IoT Analytics as a consumption-based service for cost-effectiveness. For example, AWS IoT Analytics is a fully-managed IoT analytics service that collects, pre-processes, enriches, stores and analyses IoT device data. AWS customers can also bring their custom analysis packaged in a container to execute AWS IoT Analytics. This Public Cloud offering can be beneficial to deal with the cost of the solutions for our digital transformation initiatives.

As transformation architects, we also need to focus on the representation of data available to our consumers in visually compelling formats. For example, our consumers can use analytics to make sense of data, such as key performance indicators in the visualisation application in dashboards. These dashboards can include risk management views, errors, bottlenecks and view the Internet of Things in real-time.

Considering Data Lakes for IoT Data

We covered the data lakes in previous chapters; hence we don't go into the details in this section. However, it is essential to highlight that IoT introduces new ways to collect data from various real-time data sources coming from the sensors of connected devices such as smart products, vehicles, and many other devices across the enterprise. This massive data creates a challenge for data management practice and platforms.

To address this challenge, using a data lake for IoT generated rich data makes it easier to store and perform analytics for IoT data.

The speed of using clean data (aggregated in a single place) for analytics can help discover ways to reduce operational costs and increase the quality of data. To this end, we need to aggregate IoT data sets in a single centralised place like data lakes.

IoT Architectural Challenges for Business

There are several challenges related to IoT solutions in digital transformation initiatives. The challenges are multiple angles, such as architectural, technical, and non-technical. The most common architectural challenges for IoT are mobility, scalability, capacity, extendibility, interoperability, network bottlenecks, and connectivity.

Mobility is a common IoT Architecture Non-Functional aspect affecting the solutions across the enterprise and transformation programs. IoT devices need to move a lot and change their IP address and networks frequently based on their locations. For example, the routing protocols, such as RPL, must reconstruct the DODAG (Destination Oriented, Directed Acyclic Graph) each time a node goes off the network or joins the network, which adds substantial overhead. These granular technical details, which concern mobility, may have a severe impact on solution performance, availability, security, and cost in our transformation programs.

IoT solutions for digital transformation require overall scalability and capacity plans. IoT applications integrate with and serve multiple devices in the ecosystem. Managing the distribution of devices across networks and the enterprise application landscape can be complicated.

We may need a dynamic increase or decrease in capacity, coupled with vertical and horizontal scalability and extendibility of the solutions in the enterprise. IoT applications need to be tolerant of new services and devices joining the network at a fast speed. Addressing this challenge requires dynamic scalability and enormous extendibility.

Interoperability means that heterogeneous devices, solution components, elements, and protocols need to be able to work with each other harmoniously. Maintaining the interoperability in an IoT ecosystem is another challenge owing to the wealth of platforms, solution components, devices and protocols used in IoT ecosystems.

Network bottlenecks adversely affect availability, performance and the cost of products or services in productions, making the service level agreements challenging to meet. Apart from latency related to the distance, several other factors are causing the network bottlenecks. Some common causes of network bottlenecks are malfunctioning devices, having an excessive number of devices connected to the networks, limited bandwidth, and overcapacity for server utilisation.

Several other considerations also need to be made when it comes to internet connectivity related to IoT solutions in our digital transformation programs; for example, the type of Internet services, internet service providers, usage cost, and communication speed.

IoT Security and Privacy Concerns

The major IoT concerns revolve around security and privacy for the enterprise. IoT technologies are rapidly-changing, expanding and transforming to different functions and shapes; hence, IoT technologies can have a tremendous impact on security.

The previous security solutions may not meet newer solutions for the enterprise. We need fresh security approaches to address new risks, issues, and dependencies. A recent addition to IoT security is the integration of blockchain to create secure and reliable connections.

Blockchain enables the smart IoT devices to control, monitor and automate using the secure and reliable approach. Consideration of Blockchain for the digital transformation initiatives may be beneficial to address security and privacy concerns as we mentioned in the security section in the technology chapter.

Privacy is related to security. It is well-known that security risks can cause privacy issues. IoT privacy concerns are complex and complicated due to their nature; that is, they vary from country to country and are not always overt or obvious.

Therefore, to begin with, as transformation architect, we need to pay special attention to privacy requirements at the program level. Then, applying architectural rigours, such as adding privacy concerns to the architectural assessment and applying stringent risk management and mitigation process, can be very useful to address privacy concerns in our digital transformation goals.

Chapter 12: High Performing Teams for Digital Transformation

Purpose

A digital ecosystem can be consisting of many interrelated teams with a wide variety of professionals covering various facets of digital transformation programs. We can come across many roles and responsibilities in these programs.

These roles and responsibilities need to be known and understood clearly. Stakeholder management is one of the primary responsibilities of transformation architects in digital transformation programs.

Understanding team structures, dynamics and many roles and responsibilities require a considerable amount of effort and organisation. Let's discuss these significant factors in subsequent sections starting with the talent as a crucial enabler of digital transformations.

Digital Transformation Talent

Talent is essential in digital transformation initiatives. Therefore, as business architects, we need to understand the value and importance of talent for our digital transformation programs. Without calibre talent, our digital transformation programs cannot progress and transform productively.

To this end, we need to be very cautious to nurture and keep talent in our teams. We need to make every effort to retain valuable talent in our teams. We cannot emphasise enough that talent is a crucial enabler of core products and services of modernising and transforming enterprises. Without talent, an organisation cannot be competitive in its digital transformation goals. There is a constant talent hunting in the industry to secure these scarce resources.

As business architects in our programs, we need to perform talent management and facilitation roles. We can encourage the architecting team members, especially less junior team members to perform better and turn them into talented team players.

We can also pick up poor performance in our programs and help remove poorly performing employees and replace them with talented team members who can genuinely contribute to the digital transformation vision. Our success depends on high-performance teams consisting of talented members.

Team Performance

Digital transformation initiatives require team members who can perform and produce at the highest possible level. These team members must perform optimally at all times to meet the challenges of these programs. Their skills and capabilities must be tested and validated to suit the type of work they are performing in our programs.

Building high-performance teams are critical for the success of our programs. We need to create proactive and engaged local technical teams and community of practices as give back activities. These high-quality teams and collaborative community of practices can generate innovative, high-quality solutions in an accelerated manner. They are ideal contributors to digital transformation goals.

As our teams are involved in complex digital transformation matters, people may have blind spots to understand the sophisticated dynamics. Blind spots can be hazardous in digital endeavours. The owner of the blind spot cannot see his or her blind spot unless using specific tools or assistance from someone else who is more experienced.

Habits and habitual thinking patterns are common causes of blind spots. Focusing on details without seeing the big picture can also cause cloudy thinking and ultimately dangerous blind spots.

However, as astute business architects, we need to look for big pictures from multiple angles and deep dive when needed hence can quickly identify blind spots and weaknesses experienced by our team members in our transformation programs.

We need to articulate situations with constructive feedback, lots of clarifying examples, metaphors, and similes. This influential articulation focus can help people to see their blind spots, understand their weaknesses, and turn them into strengths. Related to blind spots, identifying hidden agendas and hidden costs are critical for digital transformation initiatives.

Taking necessary performance measures are essential in our transformation programs. We need to focus on both qualitative and quantitative measures for team success. We can manage across complex matrix structures in our organisations to integrate skills to our programs.

As metric oriented architects, we need to use KPIs (Key Performance Indicators). We can use a team dashboard to see the trends and qualify and quantify progress in visual formats for the team members and the business stakeholders.

We need to encourage other team members to create their dashboard and shared dashboard for the team in our transformation programs. Our teams must turn our program to a data-driven organisation to measure the progress of digital transformation goals structurally and methodically.

One of the key measures is customer orientation and support mechanisms. We ensure a customer-centric outlook is provided, focusing on continually improving client experience with measurable results. We are expected to be the 'thought leaders' in our digital transformation programs. Thought leadership is a critical need and demand in digital transformation environments, for changing cultures, and transforming ecosystems.

Tangible outcomes are essential for the success of digital transformation programs. These programs require tangible outcomes iteratively rather than monolithic. For example, some tangible outcomes can be a virtualisation of platforms, creating containers, creating reusable shared resources, reviewed products, and agreed services.

As business architects, we need to pay special attention to providing measurable outcomes with the support of our architecting team members. Transforming business environments present constant and rapid changes. We know that any change matters in the digitally transforming ecosystem.

These small and rapid changes lead to more significant measurable outcomes at later stages of the digital transformation initiatives; for example, the systems may need to be fully automated, loosely coupled, service-oriented, software-defined, self-learning, self-managing, and self-healing are a few to mention in this context. Now that we emphasised the importance and approach for team performance let's get to know our key players from the architectural point of view in our programs.

Technical Professionals for Transformation

As business architects, we work with many technical professionals involved in digital initiatives in our programs. For example, we closely work with architects, designers, and technical specialists. At the highest level, we work with the enterprise architects applying a rigorous enterprise architecture approach to help us with digital transformation initiatives. Let's beware that if the business and enterprise architecture process go wrong in dealing with a digital transformation initiative, everything else goes wrong in our digital transformation programs.

All other architecture types, such as solution architecture, system architecture, integration architecture, and other architecture domains, are all dependent on the quality of business and enterprise architecture. Apart from architecture, the subsequent activities in the digital transformation lifecycle are also adversely affected.

After a validated, business-focused, and pragmatic architecture supporting the digital transformation strategy, the design (both high level and detailed level) is the next vital aspect to be considered in the lifecycle.

As business architects, we participate in various forums such as the Architecture Review Boards and Design Authority forums. These forums are consisting of many architects, designers and technical specialists. For example, a Design Authority maybe consist of multiple architects with diverse expertise in different domains. Usually, enterprise architects orchestrate the activities with their broad knowledge and understanding of the strategy, architecture, technical matters, and business. They govern the Design Authority by using their organisational skills coupled with other architectural skills and business understanding. Enterprise architects heavily rely on business architects to understand business stakeholder dynamics. Let's understand the role of enterprise architects as we must work with them day to day basis in our digital transformation programs.

Enterprise Architects

Enterprise Architects have strategic, architectural thinking, and design thinking skills. These esteemed architects need to articulate the current enterprise environment to the sponsoring senior executives, set future enterprise environment goals, and show how to bridge the gap for digital transformation goals between these two environments.

At a high level, Enterprise Architects understand the overall digital transformation scope, requirements, and use cases of the solutions. Besides, Enterprise Architects perform Viability Assessments which are critical to our digital transformation programs. These architects must regularly assess risks, issues, dependencies and constraints considering strengths, weaknesses, opportunities and threats in their day to day tasks.

Enterprise Architects are responsible and accountable for architectural and technical governance. Technical governance is an essential aspect of digital transformation initiatives. These programs require particular governance model due to their nature. A dynamic and flexible governance model is essential for digital transformation initiatives. The traditional stringent and extreme rule-based oppressive governance models can be roadblocks to the progress. Agility principles best suit to the dynamic governance models.

Enterprise Architects usually perform the role of technical governance head in sizeable digital transformation programs. They can have formal governance roles. For example, these architects can run the architecture review boards or design authority forums established for complex digital transformation programs.

Domain Architects

Domain Architects usually assigned to a specific business domain and play various roles and responsibilities in digital transformation programs.

Domain Architects can architect a component or integrated component in their business units. Even though they are business focussed, they can also have a strong technical background covering various aspects of architecture such as infrastructure, applications, data, security and more.

When we are working for a specific business unit problem, these domain architects can be instrumental in providing required guidance to our initiatives.

Infrastructure Architects

Infrastructure Architects are responsible for the underlying infrastructure such as network, servers, storage, platforms, physical facilities such as data centres and communications.

These architects are responsible for the plumbing of the digital world. As transformation architects, we closely work with Infrastructure Architects as they are astute about the infrastructure components of our digital initiatives.

Application Architects

Application Architects are responsible for applications and middleware across the enterprise. Enterprises can have many standalone and integrated applications spanning across multiple servers, domains and geographic locations.

Application Architects understand the functionality, operability, supportability, integration, and migration of applications.

As transformation architects, we closely work with Application Architects. They are critical resources for digital transformation programs.

Specialist Architects

This may sound like a misnomer, but there are undoubtedly specialist level architects. Even though architects cover breadth, some architects specialise in particular areas in the enterprise due to the extensive scope of the domains.

The most common specialty areas for architects are Security Architect, Data Architect, Information Architect, Network Architect, Mobility Architect, Workplace Architect.

Some of these types of architects can also serve as a subject matter experts or technical specialists which we cover in the next section.

Technical Specialists

As transformation architects, we work closely with technical specialists who have distinct technology expertise covering a broad spectrum of technologies in all technical domains. These specialists are technically eminent professionals in their chosen field. In some organisations, they are called distinguished specialists.

Technical eminence or distinguished refers to outstanding technical expertise recognised internally and externally to the organisation of a technical leader who is influential and high impact to both technical and business communities.

Some technical specialists have strong industry skills, demonstrate thought leadership, and possess multiple domain expertise. These specialists are highly regarded and sought after for their views and contributions to digital transformation initiatives.

Leading our digital transformation programs requires distinguishing technical factors in multiple technology domains with in-depth understanding to some extent. These groups of people are ideal talents for our digital transformation programs.

Business Analysts

Even though they are not technical, we closely work with the Business Analysts in architecting. Business Analysts are critical resources to translate business requirements to technical requirements working with business stakeholders, domain architects, and technical specialists.

Exceptional communication skills are essential for Business Analysts dealing with digital transformation initiatives. Their communication skills are well respected and sought after by their peers, managers, and customers.

Business Analysts are expected to communicate at all levels with confidence and ease. They must articulate the most complex situations and technical matters to all stakeholders in a language that those people can understand. Business Analysts must customise their messages based on audience profile.

Business Architects as Mentors and Coaches

Mentoring and coaching is a cultural shift and the essential requirement of modernising and digitally transforming environments. There must be a constant nurturing and knowledge transfer from top to bottom.

To this end, as business architects, we must be mentors for our team members, other team members, people from partnering organisations, students from universities, and even external people in other organisations.

We need to generously share our knowledge and transfer them to anyone who needs such knowledge to utilise in digital transformation engagements.

We also need to be good at coaching our peers, subordinates, and cross-team members by being a soundboard to them. Junior team members can be easily overwhelmed by the rapid pace changes and challenges of transformation programs.

We can be excellent listeners and even contribute to the wellbeing of our team members providing coaching sessions for stressful colleagues resulting in therapeutic outcomes. Digital transformation teams experience an enormous amount of stress, especially with accelerated delivery for growing stakeholder and consumer demands.

Business Architects ad Agile and Change Champions

Change is inevitable in digital transformation programs. Everything in these programs changes continuously and rapidly. Change leadership is a vital function for digital transformation initiatives. Dealing with rapid change is non-trivial, and indeed require delicate skills, experience, and insights.

As business architects, we must be catalysts for ongoing change and serve as an Agile Champion. With our catalytical contributions, we need to refresh the culture to more agile, collaborative, inventive, and innovative landscapes in our programs.

As change and agile champion, we can create innovative sets of practices in the transforming ecosystem. Our attributes, such as being responsive, sharing and learning mutually, and having fun with joy in a pleasant team environment, can have a tremendous impact on improving the culture for positive change in our transformation programs.

Team Learning

Learning is a never-ending process in transformational environments leading towards modernisation of legacy enterprise and digitally transforming business programs. Due to changing technology stacks, process, and tools, as transformation architects, we need to learn rapidly and efficiently.

We can have a wide variety of learning styles. Based on situations and conditions, we need to learn formally and informally based on circumstances. We need to turn every possible interaction to a potential learning opportunity in our programs.

We must create learning opportunities only for ourselves but also for team members in the program. We also need to teach other people actively and on-demand. By teaching our team members, we can even learn more and better. This new way of learning is critical to meet the demands of transformation goals.

Chapter 13: Importance of Reuse and Repeat for Digital Transformation

Purpose

The purpose of this chapter is to highlight the importance of reuse and repeat within the digital transformation program.

Importance of Repeat

Digital transformation lifecycle is recursive with successive steps and results. There is no end to digital transformation. Therefore, it is a program rather than a project. We may complete a cycle, but as soon as its completion we need to deal with another transformation cycle.

As time passes, business change directions, new business requirements emerge, business systems get older; technology stacks become obsolete, business processes get convoluted and unusable; just like human beings, everything ages in the ecosystem. Therefore, we always need to modernise and transform our business ecosystem including processes, tools and technology stacks.

Due to this natural phenomenon, I added the repeat step to our digital transformation method. However, from an architectural and architecting perspective, the repeat process needs to be well structured based on a dynamic lifecycle management process.

Importance of Asset Reuse

As business architects, we can re-use our business architectural frameworks and technical design assets multiple times as needed. The main reason for this is to save time and reduce the cost of rework. In addition, using established and validated building blocks of our architectural solutions can be very powerful to maintain and increase the quality requirements coming from our business stakeholders.

The most commonly used architectural assets are the reference architectures. Let's touch on reference architecture in the subsequent section.

Reference Architectures

A reference architecture is a re-usable business solution or a technical design in a template format. The use of a reference architecture for digital transformation initiatives can save us a considerable amount of time. Reference architectures are developed by experienced architects based on successful outcomes obtained from delivered business solutions to consumers.

This means that we can trust the reference architectures as they were once successfully delivered for consumption. Following the same path as our customised specifications, these re-usable templates can save us a considerable amount of time and can improve the quality of our new solutions.

As reference architectures are developed by experienced architects, they can also guide us in dealing with the unknown aspects of the initiatives. Reference architectures can be used for various domains, can be combined to extend functionality and can be integrated for the final business architecture outcomes.

Reference architectures are developed based on the collaborative spirit in many organisations. Some architects share their experiences internally or externally for various reasons. For example, some architects share them for charitable give-back purposes or networking, or to boost their reputation and recognition in their industry. Whatever the reasons they share them, the reference architectures are invaluable resources for our planned solution architectures.

Open-source organisations produce many reference architectures in their domains. There are two primary sources for these reference architectures: either their members develop them as part of an open-source team, or some commercial companies donate their re-usable assets to the open-source organisations as reference architectures. The Open Group (TOG) is a typical example of this kind of open-source organisation.

Reference Architectures can be at a high-level or other detailed level. For example, a typical IoT reference Architecture at a high level can include essential points, such as Portal, Dashboard, API Management, Analytics, Services, Communications, Devices, Device Management, Security Management, and Infrastructure. Reference Architectures are usually represented in diagrams with minimal text to explain the representations in the diagrams. Clarity is the main factor for a reference architecture. Reference Architectures usually are easy to understand and use.

As business architects, we need to encourage our domain and solution architects to leverage available references architectures related to digital transformation initiatives. We also need to encourage them to create their reference architectures and share with other domain architects in our programs. From my experience, smart reuse of architectural assets can help reduce architecture cost substantially in the digital transformation programs.

Chapter 14: Conclusions

We reached the conclusions after covering numerous facets of business architecture, business architectural role, the relationships within the team, and all steps of our digital transformation method (DTM).

We discussed that our digital transformation method includes twelve steps. We covered each step in a distinct chapter. Let's take a quick review of the steps:

1. Establish Fundamentals

2. Simplify Complexity

3. Manage Cost

4. Innovate and Invent

5. Accelerate Delivery

6. Grow with Collaboration

7. Leverage Emerging Technology & Tools

8. Reconstruct & Modernise Data

9. Mobilise Building Blocks

10. Create Smart Objects

11. Create Digital Teams

12. Reuse and Repeat

I attempted to show significant aspects and valuable considerations for architecting digital transformation with a proven twelve-step method. I hope you found the method and the framework easy to follow and the content concise, practical, informative, and easy-to-read.

You may have experienced an overemphasis on the architectural rigour in this book which is on purpose. We cannot compromise the rigour aiming to the quality of products and services as a target outcome for digital transformation goals in the business organisations. However, there must be a delicate balance among architectural rigour, business value, and speed to market.

Applying a pragmatic architectural approach can add business value to digital transformation programs. The key point is using an incrementally progressing iterative approach to every aspect of digital transformation initiative, including people, processes, tools, and technologies as a whole.

I hope this book provided valuable insights into the unique role of business architects leading digital transformations programs.

Appendix: Other Books in this Series

A Practical Guide for IoT Solution Architects

Architecting secure, agile, economic, highly available, well-performing IoT ecosystems

The focus of this book is to provide IoT solution architects with practical guidance and a unique perspective. Solution architects working in IoT ecosystems have an unprecedented level of responsibility at work; therefore, dealing with IoT ecosystems can be daunting.

As an experienced practitioner of this topic, I understand the challenges faced by the IoT solution architects. In this book, I have reflected upon my insights based on my solution architecture experience spread across three decades. In addition, this book can also guide other architects and designers who want to learn the architectural aspects of IoT and understand the key challenges and practical resolutions in IoT solution architectures. Each chapter focuses on the key aspects that form the framing scope for this book; namely, security, availability, performance, agility, and cost-effectiveness.

In this book, I have also provided useful definitions, a brief practical background on IoT and a guiding chapter on solution architecture development. The content is mainly practical; hence, it can be applied or be a supplemental input to the architectural projects at hand.

Architecting Big Data Solutions Integrated with IoT & Cloud

Create strategic business insights with agility

IoT, Big Data, and Cloud Computing are three distinct technology domains with overlapping use cases. Each technology has its own merits; however, the combination of three creates a synergy and the golden opportunity for businesses to reap the exponential benefits. This combination can create technological magic for innovation when adequately architected, designed, implemented, and operated.

Integrating Big Data with IoT and Cloud architectures provide substantial business benefits. It is like a perfect match. IoT collects real-time data. Big Data optimises data management solutions. Cloud collects, hosts, computes, stores, and disseminates data rapidly.

Based on these compelling business propositions, the primary purpose of this book is to provide practical guidance on creating Big Data solutions integrated with IoT and Cloud architectures. To this end, the book offers an architectural overview, solution practice, governance, and underlying technical approach for creating integrated Big Data, Cloud, and IoT solutions.

The book offers an introduction to solution architecture, three distinct chapters comprising Big Data, Cloud, and the IoT with the final chapter, including conclusive remarks to consider for Big Data solutions. These chapters include essential architectural points, solution practice, methodical rigour, techniques, technologies, and tools.

Creating Big Data solutions are complex and complicated from multiple angles. However, with the awareness and guidance provided in this book, the Big Data solutions architects can be empowered to provide useful and productive solutions with growing confidence.

A Technical Excellence Framework for Innovative Digital Transformation Leadership

Transform enterprise with technical excellence, innovation, simplicity, agility, fusion, and collaboration

The primary purpose of this book is to provide valuable insights for digital transformational leadership empowered by technical excellence by using a pragmatic five-pillar framework. This empowering framework aims to help the reader understand the common characteristics of technical and technology leaders in a structured way.

Even though there are different types of leaders in broad-spectrum engaging in digital transformations, in this book, we only concentrate on excellent technical and technology leaders having digital transformation goals to deal with technological disruptions and robust capabilities to create new revenue streams. No matter whether these leaders may hold formal executive titles or just domain specialist titles, they demonstrate vital characteristics of excellent technical leadership capabilities enabling them to lead complex and complicated digital transformation initiatives.

The primary reason we need to understand technical excellence and required capabilities for digital transformational leadership in a structured context is to model their attributes and transfer the well-known characteristics to the aspiring leaders and the next generations. We can transfer our understanding of these capabilities at an individual level and apply them to our day to day activities. We can even turn them into useful habits to excel in our professional goals. Alternatively, we can pass this information to other people that we are responsible for, such as our teenagers aiming for digital leadership roles, tertiary students, mentees, and colleagues.

We attempt to define the roles of strategic technical and technology leaders using a specific framework, based on innovation, simplicity, agility, collaboration, fusion and technical excellence. This framework offers a common understanding of the critical factors of the leader. The structured analysis presented in this book can be valuable to understand the contribution of technical leaders clearly.

Admittedly, this book has a bias towards the positive attributes of excellent leaders on purpose. The compelling reason for this bias is to focus on the positive aspects and describe these attributes concisely in an adequate amount to grasp the topic so that these positive attributes can be reused and modelled by the aspiring leaders. As the other side of the coin is also essential for different insights, I plan to deal with the detrimental aspects of useless leaders in a separate book, perhaps under the lessons learned context considering different use cases for a different audience type. Consequently, I excluded the negative aspects of useless leaders in this book.

A Modern Enterprise Architecture Approach Empowered with Cloud, Mobility, IoT & Big Data

Modernise enterprise with pragmatic architecture, powerful technologies, innovative agility, and fusion

I authored this book to provide essential guidance, compelling ideas, and unique ways to Enterprise Architects so that they can successfully perform complex enterprise modernisation initiatives transforming from chaos to coherence. This is not an ordinary theory book describing Enterprise Architecture in detail. There are myriad of books on the market and in libraries discussing details of enterprise architecture.

As a practising Senior Enterprise Architect, myself, I read hundreds of those books and articles to learn different views. They have been valuable to me to establish my foundations in the earlier phase of my profession. However, what is missing now is a concise guidance book showing Enterprise Architects the novel approaches, insights from the real-life experience and experimentations, and pointing out the differentiating technologies for enterprise modernisation. If only there were such a guide when I started engaging in modernisation and transformation programs. The biggest lesson learned is the business outcome of the enterprise modernisation. What genuinely matters for business is the return on investment of the enterprise architecture and its monetising capabilities. The rest is the theory because nowadays sponsoring executives, due to economic climate, have no interest, attention, or tolerance for non-profitable ventures. I am sorry for disappointing some idealistic Enterprise Architects, but with due respect, it is the reality, and we cannot change it. This book deals with reality rather than theoretical perfection. Anyone against this view on this climate must be coming from another planet. In this concise, uncluttered and easy-to-read book, I attempt to show the significant pain points and valuable considerations for enterprise modernisation using a structured approach. The architectural rigour is still essential. We cannot compromise the rigour aiming to the quality of products and services as a target outcome. However, there must be a delicate balance among architectural rigour, business value, and speed to market. I applied this pragmatic approach to multiple substantial transformation initiatives and complex modernisations programs. The key point is using an incrementally progressing iterative approach to every aspect of digital transformation initiatives, including people, processes, tools, and technologies as a whole.

Starting with a high-level view of enterprise architecture to set the context, I provided a dozen of distinct chapters to point out and elaborate on the factors which can make a real difference in dealing with complexity and producing excellent modernisation initiatives. As eminent leaders, Enterprise Architects are the critical talents who can undertake this massive mission using their people and technology skills, in addition to many critical attributes such as calm and composed approach. They are architects, not firefighters. I have full confidence that this book can provide valuable insights and aha moments for these talented architects to tackle this enormous mission turning chaos to coherence.

Digital Intelligence: A framework to digital transformation capabilities

I authored this book because dealing with intelligence, and the digital world is a passion for me and wanted to share my passion with you. In this book, I aim to provide compelling ideas and unique ways to increase, enhance, and deepen your digital intelligence and awareness and apply them to your organisation's digital journey particularly for modernisation and transformation initiatives. I used the architectural thinking approach as the primary framework to convey my message.

Based on my architectural thought leadership on various digital transformation and modernisation engagements, with the accumulated wealth of knowledge and skills, I want to share these learnings in a concise book hoping to add value by contributing to the broader digital community and the progressing initiatives.

Rest assured, this is not a theory or an academic book. It is purely practical and based on lessons learned from real enterprise transformation and modernisation initiatives taken in large corporate environments. I made every effort to make this book concise, uncluttered, and easy-to-read by removing technical jargons for a broader audience who want to enhance digital intelligence and awareness.

Upfront, this book is not about a tool, application, a single product, specific technology, or service, and certainly not to endorse any of these items. However, this book focuses on architectural thinking and methodical approach to improve digital intelligence and awareness. It is not like typical digital transformation books available on the market. In this book, I do not cover and repeat the same content of those books describing digital transformations. My purpose is different.

What distinguishes this book from other books is that I provide an innovative thinking framework and a methodical approach to increase your digital quotient based on experience, aiming not to sell or endorse any products or services even though I mention some prominent technologies which enable digital transformation, for your digital awareness, intelligence, and capabilities.

www.ingramcontent.com/pod-product-compliance
Lightning Source LLC
Chambersburg PA
CBHW021401210526
45463CB00001B/180